"This friendly an
our closed doors
fence—and the o
desire for his kingdom to come to our own neighborhoods. Rather than guilting us into greater openness, Chris and Elizabeth paint a joyful and fruitful picture for us that generates the desire, ideas, and energy we need to boldly open the doors of our homes and our lives to those who live right around us."

Nancy Guthrie, Bible teacher and author of *Even Better than Eden*

"*Neighborhoods Reimagined* is an important, helpful, practical, and fast-paced book. We have forgotten both what Jesus has said in the Sermon on the Mount in the beatitudes and we have forgotten what it means to be neighborly. What Elizabeth and Chris have done here is show us how the greatest sermon of all time relates to everyday relationships with those right next door to you. If you really believe that God is in control (and you should) then that means he has you exactly where you are for a purpose and this excellent book is going to help you find that purpose and practice. Imagine what would be possible if we all lived with the kind of intentionality and hospitality Jesus argues for in his upside-down kingdom. Through engaging stories, witty illustrations, and down-to-earth analogies, the McKinneys have shown us a better path in how we relate to our neighbors."

Michael Graham, program director for The Keller Center for Cultural Apologetics and author of *The Great Dechurching*

"Chris and Elizabeth invite us to reimagine how the gospel impacts us and our neighborhoods alongside an insightful journey through the 'refreshing breeze' of the beatitudes. Great storytellers, Chris and Elizabeth draw the reader in with relatable experiences that normalize what it looks like to be neighbors who love Jesus. The thoughtful reflection and discussion questions at the end of each chapter provide an excellent way to put their insights into practice in community. I highly recommend *Neighborhoods Reimagined*!"

Cas Monaco, FamilyLife VP of Missiology and Gospel Engagement

"Often books about the beatitudes are focused on the individual: how do *I* live out kingdom values. But the beatitudes are at their very core interested in the life of the kingdom in community. That is, with and around our neighbors. Chris and Elizabeth McKinney give us a practically helpful and uniquely engaging vision of what the life of the kingdom could look like here 'on earth as it is in heaven.' Imagine what our neighborhoods would be like if we reimagined them from Jesus' great sermon."

Jeremy Writebol, pastor of Woodside Bible Church, MI and author of *Pastor, Jesus is Enough*.

CHRIS & ELIZABETH MCKINNEY

Foreword by
Heather Holleman

NEIGHBORHOODS REIMAGINED

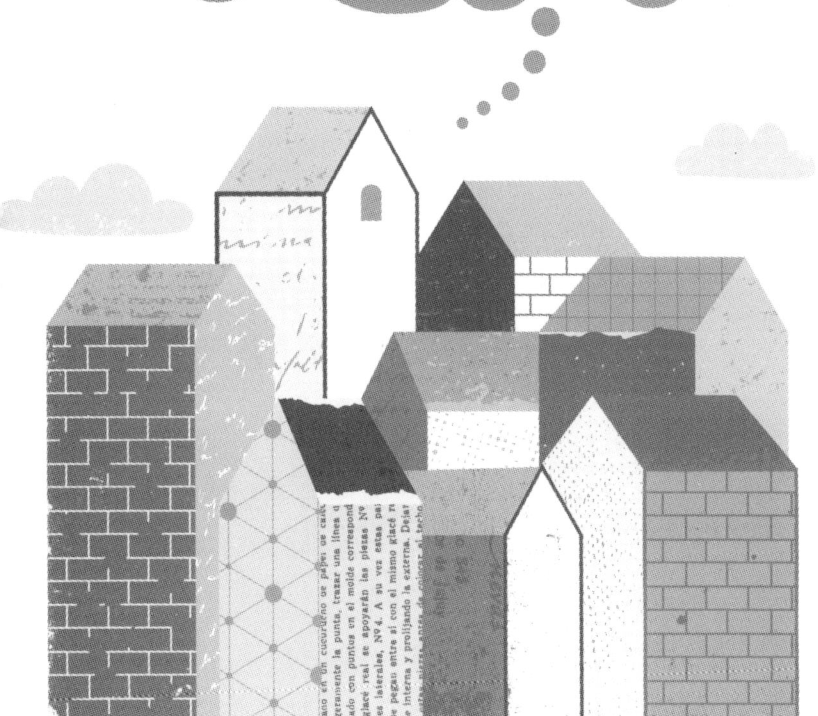

How the Beatitudes Inspire our Call to be Good Neighbors

10 Publishing
a division of 10 of those.com

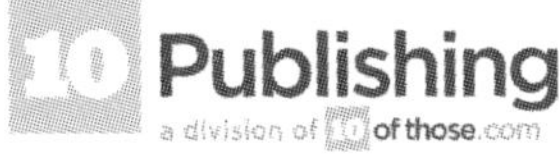

British Library Cataloguing in Publication Data
A record for this book is available from the British Library

ISBN: US: 978-1-915705-39-6
UK: 978-1-915705-14-3

Designed by Jude May
Cover image © Shanina | iStock

Printed in Denmark

10Publishing, a division of 10ofthose.com
Unit C, Tomlinson Road, Leyland, PR25 2DY, England
Email: info@10ofthose.com
Website: www.10ofthose.com

1 3 5 7 10 8 6 4 2

Blessed is the one who lives in Oxford, Ohio, generously giving her life away to college students for the sake of Christ. She will have a deep walk with God, run on four hours of sleep, and always have plenty to give away. Yep Jane, we're talking about you.

The stories in this book are based on real-life events. However, to protect the privacy and identities of the individuals involved, all names and identifying details have been altered.

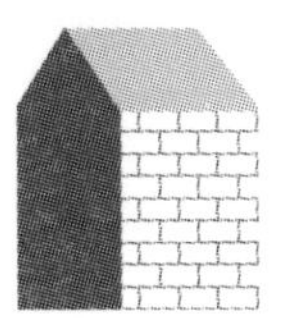

Contents

FOREWORD

When I first connected with Chris and Elizabeth McKinney, I immediately recognized our mutual passion for loving our neighbors and building the kind of communities that flourish. They inspire me, not just with their theology of neighboring, but with their genius ideas of how to *actually gather* people together. They are the kind of people I want to sit and learn from. They're smart, funny, and generous with their lives, and if you're living in their neighborhood, you'll find yourself getting a taste of the *shalom* we're all seeking. And it starts with reimagining how life could be if lived dependently on Jesus and radically interdependently with others. It starts with thinking about where we live and the people around us. It starts with living like Jesus invites us to—most notably through his words in the often-quoted and preached Sermon on the Mount. What if we applied these words in a fresh way to how we live in our neighborhoods? Imagine rewriting the cultural script of loneliness, incivility, materialism, and selfishness into a new narrative of joyful, biblical living with others.

What I didn't realize at the time of our first meeting was just how carefully this couple had thought through a biblical approach to *how* to love others well, using what they aptly call the "refreshing breeze of the beatitudes." As I began reading *Neighborhoods Reimagined*, I found myself journeying alongside Chris and Elizabeth as they disentangle themselves from a toxic cultural narrative and embrace a startling understanding of the "good life." With heart-warming personal stories and an accessible, authentic written voice, they demonstrate a way to flourish that turns us from living like self-assured, numbed-out, revenge-seeking, faith-hiding neighbors into ones that foster the unusual, counter-cultural values depicted in the Sermon on the Mount. You'll read this book and discover fresh insight into how the strange and upside-down words in the beatitudes apply to ordinary neighborhood living.

As you read each chapter and ponder the excellent reflection, prayer, and discussion prompts, you'll find yourself, as I did, carefully considering a new set of values. You'll want to love others well, right where you live, fully dependent on Jesus. Chris and Elizabeth don't shy away from the hard questions, either. What does it mean to live poor in spirit? To mourn? To live an undivided, authentic life? And what about persecution part? As you enter into each chapter, you'll find ways to live differently. You might find yourself led by God's Spirit, as the McKinney family were, to host wonderful gatherings—whether a street party, a neighborhood jog ahead of Thanksgiving, or even a tree planting party. You might find yourself driving neighbors to the hospital or supporting those enduring mental health challenges, divorce, or a devastating loss. You might become a lonely neighbor's only source of physical touch through a hug or handshake. You'll suddenly want to make space in the day for conversations with neighbors, not out of duty or guilt, but because it's the pathway to a joyfully biblical way of life together in community.

As you finish this book, you'll think about a different way to live. You'll bring to God your lack of energy, busy schedule, and numb heart, and you'll find he can work through you to do impossible, Spirit-filled things—things as simple but life-changing as walking across the street to get to know your neighbor.

Heather Holleman, PhD, professor, speaker and author of *The Six Conversations: Pathways to Connecting in an Age of Isolation and Incivility*

INTRODUCTION

How the Beatitudes and Neighboring Go Together

Breakups are never fun. Chances are, you've been through at least one in your life, and whether you were the dumper or the dumpee—the one ghosting or being ghosted—it had to be done.

Before we were married, we both went through our fair share of breakups. Our favorite is the time I (Chris) had to endure the insufferable goodbye-drive to the airport after "letting someone go." To ease the awkward silence, I turned on the radio to a cruel joke: Coldplay's "The Scientist." You know—the one where Chris Martin agonizes over how hard it is to part ways, and how no one had ever prepared us for how difficult it could be.

I can laugh about it now …

Some breakups are mutual, some one-sided, some ugly, and some out of leftfield. Sometimes you are looking for different things and just decide to "work on yourselves" and "see other people."

"It's not you, it's me."
"You're gonna make someone really happy someday."
"We can still be friends, right?"

But it's not just teenagers. Somewhere along the way, as a society, we culturally broke up with our neighbors, the next-door ones. It wasn't sudden or premeditated; it may even have been an accident. It just kind of happened. You could say it was mutual, but we never said it out loud. Life got busy; work got crazy. There was no bad blood. We just kind of drifted apart and now we haven't spoken for years.

A neighborly breakup happened at some point. It isn't just a feeling, it's a fact.

In 2005, a Georgetown University study found that 47 percent of Americans knew almost none of their neighbors.[1] Thirteen years later in 2018, the number of people who knew only a few or even none of their neighbors' names climbed to 68 percent.[2] And no doubt we will all recognize the spike in the post-2020 graph.

We said there's no bad blood, but that's not entirely true. There's some mistrust. The truth is, as we've grown apart, the social fabric of our neighborhoods has torn and frayed. Trust has waned to the point where we now feel a sense of panic when there's a knock at the door (*Quick—Hide!*). We have bigger peep holes and more sophisticated doorbells, complete with security cameras and smart speakers.

Research confirms our newly installed trust issues. Surveys say less than half of us trust our next-door neighbors and those in the youngest demographic, ages 18–29, check in at an even higher rate of 61 percent.[3] We no longer value introductions, and without having names and relationships to buffer our urban and suburban differences, we get awkward and can't find common ground. We assume nearby strangers are strange, and we stick to our inner circle and social media tribe.

Our political and social climate has further exacerbated things even more. We're so entrenched in our viewpoints that we consider it exhausting to listen to another perspective. It's tough to stay engaged when our neighbor drops political no-no's into casual conversation at the mailbox. Big issues have called for big fences, and they're so tall now we can barely see over them. As a culture at large, we've decided it might just be better for everyone if we all minded our own business and left our neighbors alone.[4]

We would never say these next-door strangers have become our next-door enemies—we just ignore them. But Jesus said that's what religious people do to those they don't really love (Lk. 10:30–37). He pointed out that even the churchiest-of-the-churchy put in their Airpods when faced with those they consider non-neighbors. So, if being more religious isn't the pathway to better neighboring, what is?

Move that Bus

Since no one really knows who discovered Chip and Joanna Gaines, let's just say I (Elizabeth) did. I was *for sure* one of the first to watch their HGTV show *Fixer Upper* when it initially aired, and I remember telling Chris I had two new best friends. But it's not just Joanna's flair for design, Chip's mad carpentry skills, or even their dynamic relationship that makes it a compelling show. There's a single story we love in every episode and the million others like it. *Property Brothers, Flip or Flop, Love It or List It*—they're all versions of the same home-reno fairytale we've been watching for over twenty years now. There's one playbook and it gets us every gosh-darn time.

First, we do the walk-through of the house in crisis. There's clutter, water damage, mold, and termites. We're convinced no one can turn this wretched space into something functional, let alone beautiful. Cue my favorite, the virtual tour. We marvel at the impossible vision the host presents. How could they have even imagined *this* from *that*? We're mesmerized, but by faith we believe. The design meeting wraps up. The host turns to the homeowners and smiles: "Let's get to work!" Off they go.

You know what comes next: demo and problems. The foundation is crumbling, the electrical wiring needs to be totally replaced, and the HVAC ducts need to be rerouted. Inevitably, as these problems arise, the homeowners get irritable. When they take their frustrations out on the host, their grievances are met with reassurance that they're right on track. They're gently reminded to refocus their hope on the future vision of their remodeled home.

Finally, the big reveal. We channel the homeowners' nerves and excitement. Our eyes are closed and the host asks if we're ready to see our fixer upper. The house is blocked by a huge picture of its original state—or a massive automobile—and we chant, "Move that bus!" And then … Our minds and hearts can't handle the shock of seeing the remodeled home in all its glory. All the stress is behind us, we can't even remember what it was like before. It's restored to its original beauty, it's better. It's as it ought to be.

Different Strokes

Early on in Matthew's Gospel, Jesus preaches the Sermon on the Mount, three stunning chapters that open with the beatitudes—

eight pithy statements laying out the qualities Jesus is looking for in his followers along with the blessings they'll bring. In the beatitudes, Jesus gives us a virtual tour of what life can be like once the bus is moved. And while they're meant to be applied to all areas of our life, over the next eight chapters we're going to specifically imagine how our neighborhoods could change if the beatitudes were lived out right where we are, right now. Jesus is lifting our eyes and giving us a better vision for what could happen if his renewing and transforming work were to come home with us.

In doing so, he knows the broad, sweeping obstacles we face in our neighborhoods. He sees the general ruin and disrepair. He understands the specific and unique challenges of our individual addresses—the isolation, independence, social anxiety, over-scheduling, suspicion, inattentiveness, and other seemingly insurmountable hurdles. But he has plans.

Just picture it: long shadows cast on a scenic, sunlit mountainside covered in wildflowers and laced with olive trees. A gentle breeze meandering through the murmurs of the crowd, stretching toward the Sea of Galilee in the distance. Jesus is about to give us the first eight verses of what many would call the greatest sermon of all time.

Are you ready? ... Drumroll, please! ... Here it comes, the big reveal ...

Blessed are the poor in spirit,
  for theirs is the kingdom of heaven.
Blessed are those who mourn,
  for they will be comforted.
Blessed are the meek,
  for they will inherit the earth.

> Blessed are those who hunger and thirst for righteousness,
> for they will be filled.
> Blessed are the merciful,
> for they will be shown mercy.
> Blessed are the pure in heart,
> for they will see God.
> Blessed are the peacemakers,
> for they will be called children of God.
> Blessed are those who are persecuted because of righteousness,
> for theirs is the kingdom of heaven (Mt. 5:3–10).

(Crickets)

We are crestfallen. *Seriously?!* That's the big reveal? We're dumbfounded. These renderings are not the ones we expect or have our hearts set on. These are … *different*. R. T. France highlights just how different: "Imagine a different world, different identity, different set of practices, different relationship to the status quo."[5]

Jesus' blueprints are all upside-down and backwards.

Dale Allison says: "the beatitudes were intended to startle."[6] Startled is one way to put it. How could Jesus think this upside-down vision would be the means to restoring glory and beauty to our neighborhoods? They're nice teachings (if you could do them) but don't they seem a little pie-in-the-sky-esque? Jesus didn't think so. He offered them as a way of life meant to be lived out in nitty-gritty ways in our local communities.[7]

Jesus is introducing us to a radical new vision for what it means to be human.[8] He's presenting a countercultural view to what we've learned in the world, and possibly in our Christian subcultures as well. They are "not ideas to strive to attain or formulas for power, rather descriptions of a kind of people characteristic of the new age."[9] They are the characterizing markers of a faith rooted in Jesus.

The beatitudes are both the vision and the pathway to seeing the renewing and transforming work of Christ's kingdom come more and more to our neighborhoods. In *your* neighborhood. However upside-down this way of living might appear, it's the way Jesus turns neighborhoods right-side-up.

The Good Life

Our newsfeeds give a health and wealth perspective on what it means to be happy and #blessed. We find ample humble brags about romantic island getaways, new cars, a heroic significant other, skincare regimens, and family Easter pics—you know, *the good life*.

The good life philosophy goes back to Socrates. It's a life in which we're living in the nicest neighborhoods with the best school districts, right beside a beautiful park. We are talking high on comfort, low on problems. There's a measure of pleasure—even luxury, fulfillment, and meaning. It's a don't-worry-be-happy life that can be earned and achieved, we think. But no. Though it's easier said than done, we must disentangle from these worldly #goals though they run so deep in our culture.

In contrast to these worldly ways, Jesus offers an alternative understanding of what it means to live the good life. As Jonathan Pennington puts it, these are "wisdom invitations to the kind of life that will experience flourishing … though they seem profoundly non-flourishing in nature."[10] These blessings are not rewards we earn for right behavior. They are the route of heart-formation that will take place when we reorient ourselves as neighbors who identify with the ways of Jesus.

Grace and virtue are not enemies; they're best friends. We are not redeemed by the beatitudes, but the beatitudes show we've been redeemed.

David paints a picture of the kind of unexpected flourishing we find in living Jesus' way:

> Blessed is the one
> who does not walk in step with the wicked
> or stand in the way that sinners take
> or sit in the company of mockers,
> but whose delight is in the law of the Lord,
> and who meditates on his law day and night.
> That person is like a tree planted by streams of water,
> which yields its fruit in season
> and whose leaf does not wither—
> whatever they do prospers (Ps. 1:1–3).

What if you and I were like this flourishing, fruit-bearing, shade-making tree in our neighborhoods? What if our neighbors were attracted to the fruit and shade of Christ in our lives? What if they saw us live out this kind of "different" and flourish with a poverty of spirit? Would it cause them to be curious about Christ for once ... or again?

Would it challenge their thinking to see a Christian neighbor flourish in an all-together different kind of way? What if our neighbors saw that Jesus made a difference in how we think about our politics? Or the way we talk about our bosses? What if they were to see meekness and peace in us? What if entitlement and rage were missing? Would they think we were living our best lives?

If your neighbors had a bird's eye view into your living room or kitchen, would they see this alternative good life?

Our Story

When we moved into our home eleven years ago, we never set out to write a book on neighboring. We were quite fine hunkering down like everyone else around us. Except that we weren't fine. In truth, we were in one of the most stressful seasons of our life and it was really our neediness that prompted us to consider connecting with those in our proximity. This in turn, led us to the conundrum of how to meet "said neighbors," since we were all so isolated. We needed an excuse … ours was a fish fry. That's when something special happened—though we hardly recognized it at the time—we went from side-by-side strangers to acquaintances, the first step.

What started as a little get-together with a few couples, became a tradition for our little suburban subdivision and grew over the years to include five streets and a few cul-de-sacs. Now yearly when the weather gets nice, we gather as singles, empty-nesters, young parents, toddlers and teens—everyone showing up outside our home with a big appetite and food to share. Some are holding newborns, some swapping health sagas, some making TikTok videos; all feeling like we're a part of one big family. The fish fry became the first of many excuses we've made to hang out and build relationships with those around us. Whether through hot sauce nights, yard sales, egg hunts, or our walking school bus, we've grown close to neighbors across generations, racial demographics, and worldviews. We've sought the common good of the neighborhood together and seen our community come alive.

It felt vulnerable at first, though. After all, no one had appointed us the mayors of our neighborhood. But as we pushed through obstacles and insecurities, we found that most neighbors were just waiting for someone else to make the first move. Over time, what began as casual connections at a yard sale or neighborhood clean-up day evolved into deeper friendships that could bear much weightier conversations … conversations about struggle and loss and purpose and God. We started to see some neighbors try church on for size and some begin to follow Jesus. Not every neighbor has been baptized or is even spiritually interested of course, but God is at work on these five streets, we can tell you that.

Aha Moment

On the heels of Jesus' beatitude vision, comes a familiar passage:

> *You are the salt of the earth*. But if the salt loses its saltiness, how can it be made salty again? It is no longer good for anything, except to be thrown out and trampled underfoot.
> *You are the light of the world*. A town built on a hill cannot be hidden. Neither do people light a lamp and put it under a bowl. Instead they put it on its stand, and it gives light to everyone in the house. In the same way, *let your light shine before others, that they may see your good deeds and glorify your Father in heaven* (Mt. 5:13–16, emphasis added).

I (Elizabeth) was already sold on the idea that each follower of Christ has been placed in a particular neighborhood to serve him there, but when Chris initially proposed the idea of writing a book about neighboring and the beatitudes, I wasn't so sure. The language felt unfamiliar and intimidating to me. Words like poor, hungry, and persecuted were ones I'd rather avoid than write a book about. Overall, I feared we'd be out over our skis with a passage too difficult to understand, let alone apply.

But I had an "aha moment" when I discovered that the well-known and beloved salt and light passage immediately followed these strange, upside-down phrases on kingdom blessing.[11] I felt convicted that if I wanted to grow in showing and sharing the love of Jesus in a bright and salty way, it would serve me well to back up twelve verses to the beginning of Matthew 5. So, Chris and I dived in together and both became convinced that these beatitude renderings are not only the roadway Jesus gives for our flourishing, but for living as salt and light in our dark and flavorless world.

And we can begin right in the place we're arguably our most authentic selves: at home. Whether your neighborhood consists of five streets in the suburbs like ours, five homes in the outskirts, or five stories in the city, you've been placed for a purpose and your context is unique. Maybe your closest neighbor is a mile away or maybe they're living right above you and you can hear them shuffling about as you're reading this page. Whether you're rather spread out, all crammed into the same building, or somewhere in-between, God has placed you to bring salt and light right where you are.

We Can't Even

But before you go making beatitude banners and hanging these adages on your bathroom walls, we should ask—have you tried to be merciful for an hour? Is meekness or mourning your cup of tea?

In a way, we're all kind of like those awkward television singing-competition contestants, and no one (not even Mom) has the heart to tell us that we're unprepared, unqualified, and just don't have what it takes to live out this opening section in the fifth chapter of the book of Matthew.

If we'll listen, the beatitudes will break our hearts. In our strength, we just cannot do them. Not with our neighbors, not with anyone.

But when all hope is gone, a hidden door opens and light shines in. Jesus peeks through. He reveals himself as our true example; the fulfillment of each and every beatitude. When we find him persecuted, poor in spirit, pure in heart, and peacemaking, we will no longer despair. We will worship as we find our mourning, meek, and merciful Savior, hungering and thirsting to put right the wrongs around him.

Then, as those newly dependent on his Spirit, we'll have new eyes to see Jesus' ongoing renovation of our neighborhoods, imagining how these invitations might play out. When we get discouraged by all the obstacles and all the problems we see in ourselves and around us, that's part of the work, too. Jesus, our gracious host, comes to us in our hardhats and bootstraps, and he gently reassures us that his vision will one day be reality. He reminds us it's his work from the start. That his kingdom is advancing and will one day cover the entire world as the waters cover the seas, including the very corner of the world in which we now live, our neighborhoods. He will do it and we will live in restored and renovated neighborhoods where we wholly reflect him.

> Look! God's dwelling place is now among the people, and he will dwell with them. They will be his people, and God himself will be with them and be their God (Rev. 21:3).

As we mull over Jesus' upside-down kingdom, watch him live out each beatitude, and save us from our inability to do them ourselves, we will be transformed into new kinds of neighbors. Thankfully neither Jesus nor our neighbors expect polished, pretty, or perfect. Just you, as you are. We'll be changed by Jesus together.

But we start at the end … the end of us.

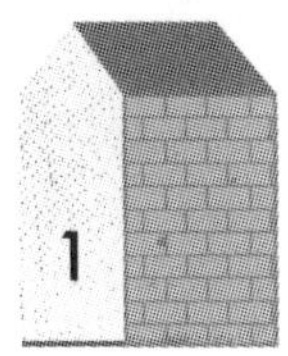

Spiritual Zeros

Jesus said: "Blessed are the poor in spirit, for theirs is the kingdom of heaven."

The world says: "Blessed are the self-assured, for they will retire early with spiritual independence."

Imagination is a good thing. Everything that exists is a product of imagination—airplanes and alarm clocks, sidewalks and sandcastles, vending machines and the internet. Before they existed, they lived in someone's mind.

Our imaginations bring hope to all the maybe and what-if possibilities that run through our heads. We can be transported to an exotic beach across the ocean simply by closing our eyes or replay a conversation with the witty remark we wish we'd said. We can see ourselves traveling the world, buying our dream home, or even just losing a few pounds. Creative juices are unlocked when we envision what it would be like to do the big thing we've talked about for years.

With the beatitudes, Jesus is inviting us to reimagine ourselves and our neighborhoods—to picture what it would look like for his kingdom values to take up residence in our hearts and our neck of the woods. These eight beatitudes are his invitations for you to see yourself and the half-mile radius around you in a whole new way. Ready? Here comes the first one, so buckle up.

You carefully tear open the envelope with one eye squinted closed. Long pause …

The first invitation is totally empty.

Insufficient Funds

Ambiance is everything, is it not? A tidy classroom, an aromatic kitchen, a candlelit dinner. What would be a fitting venue to set the tone for arguably the greatest sermon of all time? Jesus was gaining notoriety and needed somewhere he could deliver his manifesto. Matthew tells us just prior:

> News about him spread all over Syria, and people brought to him all who were ill with various diseases, those suffering severe pain, the demon-possessed, those having seizures, and the paralyzed; and he healed them. Large crowds from Galilee, the Decapolis, Jerusalem, Judea and the region across the Jordan followed him (Mt. 4:24–25).

He had the magic touch and people were taking note. He was gaining followers from every direction. It was becoming clear this wasn't some low-key thing; it was a movement. All this buzz called for a massive stage with bright lights and two massive screens, minimum … or a grassy hill. You can guess which one Jesus picked.

Amidst high-running religious tensions and messianic expectations, Jesus was setting a different kind of stage with his first beatitude. This was a mountain vision of downwardness, so to speak. If his fans were wanting in on celebrity, platform, and power, Jesus' opener had a lot of potential for side eyes and awkward silences. Just when they thought there was nowhere to go but up, all signs were pointing down. And we're talking way down.

There they were, squeezed in near some neighbors they hadn't spoken to in years, fiddling grass between their fingers, the sun in their eyes, their worldviews about to get rocked.

Imagine you're there, too. Jesus taps the microphone a few times and the sound bounces back with a high-pitched squeal. Finally, he sits down and begins: "Blessed are the poor in spirit, for theirs is the kingdom of heaven" (Mt. 5:3).

Come again? Since you've never before heard the words "poor in spirit" strung together in a sentence, it sounds like Jesus is speaking a foreign language. Why would anyone want to be poor—in spirit or in any regard for that matter—and how could spiritual brokenness be something that leads to personal and collective blessing?

In a world of haves and have-nots, this sounds like an invitation to disadvantage. Who would choose being poor over being privileged? Candidly speaking, the first blessing sounds more like a curse.

Needy Neighbors

Neighbors come in all shapes and sizes. Over the last eleven years, we've gotten to know lots of different neighbors from all different backgrounds. Atheists and agnostics, Hindus and hedonists, swingers and seekers, pantheists and palm readers, the list goes on. Our neighborhood is filled with progressives and conservatives, old and young, introverts and extroverts, partiers, busy-bodies, empty-nesters … you get it.

What are your neighbors like? If you stopped to chat for a bit after grabbing the mail, how do you imagine the conversation would flow? Would it feel clumsy? Would they dodge you? Would they be pleasantly surprised by your initiative? Perhaps they would hold you hostage and talk your ear off, ignoring social cues that your groceries are getting heavy and you're anxious to get in and let your dog out? At the end of a long day, these unknowns are a lot to navigate, especially if the neighbor is … needy.

Our culture demonizes needy people. At best they're insecure and socially unaware; at worst, they're manipulative and never satisfied. We instinctively fear neediness and dissociate ourselves from it. But before we write off this kind of vulnerability, we need to turn the spotlight on ourselves. What if we're the needy ones? And what if it's supposed to be that way? Jesus has a different gauge for being a needy neighbor and it isn't all bad.

Jesus knew what he was doing with this first beatitude. With it, he offers us a deep dive into understanding our self-lack. We started our discipleship journeys by coming to Jesus with nothing in our pockets, and being poor in spirit means we *keep* coming to God that way. We never move on from the fact that we were down and out without Christ. It's not our goal to retire early as spiritually independent. Even with all the riches of Christ now ours, there's an ongoing acknowledgment that he did all the work, and without that early inheritance transfer into our account, we'd be bad-off and spiritually broke without him.

Being poor in spirit has a lot to do with our view of the "self." It's resisting the urge to be self-supported, self-ruling, and self-sufficient; it's believing we flourish when we stay listed as dependents.

Though Jesus' first preaching point might strike us as unfortunate, it's not out of the blue. The Bible has a habit of highlighting beggars and borrowers. Inadequacy, weakness, inability, emptiness—some of Jesus' best conversation starters.

It's true. God has a thing for the weak ones. Remember Moses was not overly impressed with himself and was hyper aware of his incompetencies, Gideon thought his lowborn beginnings would make it impossible for God to use him, and Isaiah was dumbstruck when he saw how messed-up he really was. And that's just getting started. Each one held their own "Help Wanted" sign.

Rather than imagining the kingdom of heaven will come to our neighborhoods when we arrive as self-sufficient saviors with all the answers, we need to readjust our mental image and come empty-handed, having insufficient funds, and a deep God-dependence. And we stay there. In the words of the hymn writer, "Nothing in my hand I bring, simply to the cross I cling."[1]

But it's not easy.

Me Monster

A while back, we saw a comedic sketch about a "Me Monster," a narcissistic dinner guest whose favorite thing to talk about is me, myself, and I.[2] As he goes on, the comedian wants to know what it is about the human condition that likes to one-up and top people in conversations. His social fantasy involves beating the Me Monster's story with a much better one. We laugh because we can relate, both to being topped and doing the topping.

We all have an inner Me Monster. It's our first counterfeit beatitude, the version of us that believes we're self-proficient. It's why we look inside ourselves for answers, help, and resources, and the reason we posture and pretend. Me, myself, and I want to be seen as important and put-together. We love to hear ourselves talk. Listening? Not so much. Gifted, sharp, interesting—we like it. Poor, empty, needy … it's a no from me, dawg.

Our Me Monsters wonder why Jesus didn't start his sermon with something more practical, like tips about self-confidence and self-expression, to give us a better shot at becoming neighborhood influencers. In a culture where our neighbors' fences already feel so high, we feel the urge to put our very best selves forward and yet, me, myself and I stands as the biggest adversary to the first beatitude.[3]

This is where all those DIY videos maybe haven't just helped but hurt us. We can watch a five-minute YouTube tutorial on how to finish our decks, install bathroom tiles, and update our light fixtures—All. By. Ourselves. Our counterfeit beatitude persuades us: "Blessed are the self-assured, for they will retire early with spiritual independence."

Living as salt and light amongst our churched, dechurched, and unchurched neighbors however, is going to require outside help. When Jesus calls us to be poor in spirit in our neighborhoods, it involves admitting our great need to do what only he can do.

Speaking as someone who loves personality tests, I (Elizabeth) come in as an extroverted and persuasive dolphin who likes big ideas, freedom, and creativity. Chris's results reveal he's an introverted and intuitive wolf who values innovation, hard work, and loyalty. Since his parents are certified coaches in some of the more involved assessments, you can imagine our holiday dinner discussions. For those of you who resist being put in a box, it would be your worst nightmare, but we enjoy it.

Funny though how these personality appraisals are mostly designed to help us present our very best. No one would pay twenty dollars for an online test called Weakness Finder. We like to focus on our more favorable traits and get better at those, not dwell on the parts that reveal our brokenness.

So, how much does temperament play into all of this? Are some of us wired as deferential and therefore genetically predetermined to "succeed" at the beatitudes? Are some of us more likely to present as poor in spirit and others of us naturally bent toward autonomy and self-regard?

Thankfully, Jesus is talking about spirituality, not biology. A mild-mannered, polite predisposition should not be confused with a work of the Spirit.[4] Neither should a feisty bent be cause for self-elimination this early in the sermon. This kind of work cuts through nature and nurture, and offers rescue from the Me Monster for every type.

Why then, do we resist the rescuing? Unfortunately, our Me Monsters are tricky. They appear so slick, so cool, so helpful. We're convinced our own competencies can get us in the door. But over time, we realize our self-reservoirs run short.

We see this come out in our snarky comment on the neighborhood Facebook page, in our temper toward the neighbor whose trash keeps blowing in our yard, that passive-aggressive remark ready for the guy whose music keeps us up at night … and just an overall lack of love.

Whatever our default settings, left to our instincts and inner resources, we learn we're naturally neighbors who are touchy, grumpy, selfish, sometimes aggressive, sometimes indifferent. Not a great place to dig a well.

Our neighbors notice, too.

Whether it's jumping to file a neighborly dispute rather than talking face-to-face or making assumptions based on the color of our neighbor's skin or the political sign in their yard, we look a lot like the world. Our neighbors are wondering—is this really Jesus' brand?

This first beatitude invites us to begin with our arm around our Me Monster and gently say, "We don't got this."

> For I know that good itself does not dwell in me, that is, in my sinful nature. For I have the desire to do what is good, but I cannot carry it out (Rom. 7:18).

Or as the psalmist would say: "My flesh and my heart may fail, but God is the strength of my heart and my portion forever" (Ps. 73:26).

Don't know about you, but all this Weakness Finder and Me Monster talk has us a little melancholy. It's exposing and deflating to think about reimagining our neighborhoods in light of our faulty neighboring tendencies. The more we think about it, the more we realize how generally incurious we are toward the other image-bearers across the street.

We wonder how God could ever use us to show his love and light to our neighbors when we're so full of ourselves and so short of him. We need saving from our counterfeit beatitudes, we need an up-close showing of this God-dependence, and we need a new reservoir.

The Nothing Verses

As kids, a movie came out based on the German fantasy novel called *The NeverEnding Story.* The film's main antagonist is a raging storm known as The Nothing, which aims to destroy the vast, mystical universe, Fantasia. The Nothing manifests itself as a dark sky filled with swirling clouds, strong winds, lightning, and thunder. This non-being devours its enemies, leaving behind a void of nothingness.[5] The threat to take something and turn it into nothing strikes terror in its adversaries. Really, what could be scarier than … nothing?

For most of us, nothing is a dirty word. It implies loss, insignificance, and non-existence, all of which send us running because we want to be somethings and somebodies. Jesus didn't feel this way, however. Nothingness doesn't scare him in the slightest:

> [Jesus], being in very nature God, did not consider equality with God something to be used to his own advantage; rather, *he made himself nothing* (Phil. 2:6–7, emphasis added).

To describe his relationship with the Father, he spoke of himself using lots of nothings and nots:[6]

- "… the Son can do nothing by himself" (Jn. 5:19).
- "By myself I can do nothing …" (Jn. 5:30).
- "I do not accept glory from human beings …" (Jn. 5:41).
- "For I have come down from heaven not to do my will …" (Jn. 6:38).
- "My teaching is not my own" (Jn. 7:16).
- "I am not here on my own authority …" (Jn. 7:28).

- "… I do nothing on my own …" (Jn. 8:28).
- "I have not come on my own; God sent me" (Jn. 8:42).
- "I am not seeking glory for myself …" (Jn. 8:50).
- "The words I say to you I do not speak on my own authority" (Jn. 14:10).
- "These words you hear are not my own …" (Jn. 14:24).

This nothing language was his way of rejecting the world's self-relying, self-realizing, self-actualizing highways and surrendering to the all-ness of God. He wasn't afraid of embracing his neediness through a posture of moment-by-moment dependence. He yielded to God in private (Mt. 14:23), in public (Mt. 19:13), in early mornings (Mk. 1:35), and all-nighters (Lk. 6:12). He put his confidence in God in the face of sad and scary circumstances (Mt. 26:38–44), and even while dying on the cross (Mt. 27:46).

Jesus was poor in spirit but rich in Spirit.

But all this begs the question—how can we practice this posture of self-poverty in our neighborhoods? … Or can we? After all, why spend time reimagining our neighborhoods with these kingdom values if they're impossible to live out?

It is possible, but we need help.

"Lord, Help!"

A friend of ours was hired as a nanny for a two-year-old little girl, Amelia. For play time, they'd sit down on the floor and work together on one of those shape sorters—those cube-shaped early development toys covered with cut-out holes designed to fit triangles, squares, circles, and half-moons. For a toddler who's just learning, these can be extremely frustrating. Luckily for Amelia, her parents had taught her two words to say every time she needed assistance: *"Help, please."* Whenever she found herself trying to smash one of her squares into the circle-shaped hole: *Help, please.* If she was tired and her best efforts just weren't working: *Help, please.* Just didn't want to do it herself: *Help, please.*

At two years old, Amelia learned to do what so many of us never do in our relationships with God: ask for help. Inspired by this, we adapted it as a prayer to help us choose dependence over independence in even the simplest of circumstances: *"Lord, help."*

No wonder Jesus said, "Truly I tell you, unless you change and become like little children, you will never enter the kingdom of heaven" (Mt. 18:3).

Jesus knows our lack of inner resources and hasn't left us alone in this world to just do the best we can. When he was walking about on that big, grassy hill, he wasn't stooping to hand out commitment cards; he was offering little white flags. More than our efforts, he wants our dependence. Yes, being poor in spirit involves the initial confession of our spiritual bankruptcy but also the surrender and acknowledgment that we need new manna from God every day of our lives.

Jesus said, "And I will ask the Father, and he will give you another advocate to help you and be with you forever—the Spirit of truth … you know him, for he lives with you and will be in you. I will not leave you as orphans; I will come to you …" (Jn. 14:16–18).

The same Spirit that raised Jesus from the dead is alive in you (Rom. 8:11) to help you live the life you could never live apart from him. He wants to work in and through you to love your neighbors in ways you can't imagine … yet.

What does it look like to be poor in spirit where we live? The answer lies in who is doing the neighboring. Rather than see ourselves as the ones responsible for neighborhood God-growth, we know that's on him. We shift from seeing ourselves as neighborhood fruit-producers to neighborhood fruit-bearers. We don't trust our inner Me Monsters to garner relational capital or avoid our neighbors altogether. We believe that God is at work, he causes growth, and we need to stay connected to him all the time.

Do you live in a highly isolated neighborhood where no one speaks to one another, and it would feel weird to try to build relationships? *Lord, help.* Has there been bad blood between you and the neighbors ever since you did that one thing that really bothered them? *Lord, help.* Are you an introvert who hates small talk? *Lord, help.*

> I am the vine; you are the branches. If you remain in me and I in you, you will bear much fruit; apart from me you can do nothing (Jn. 15:5).

God's Spirit—not stronger bootstraps—is the answer to our big neighboring obstacles.

Do you have a job that's highly demanding, where you travel a lot and are barely home? Are you home with young kids and feel you have nothing left to give? Never given it much thought what it could look like to love your neighbors?

Lord, help.
Lord, help.
Lord, help

"Declaration of Dependence"

As the parents of four young kids, we've strived to raise daughters who tie their shoes, pick out their clothes in the morning, put their dishes away, and help with the laundry. After all, the goal of parenting is to raise independent children … right?

Our friends Jess and Alex have a daughter, Avonlea, who has a rare genetic syndrome called Cardiofaciocutaneous (CFC). She is blind, has epilepsy, is G-tube fed, and does not communicate verbally. Jess recently posted on social media:

> Adding a new level of care to Avonlea's day which at times feels we're moving backwards in her level of independence. However, it also doesn't feel sad or tragic anymore. God has given us Avonlea. Our service to her and her body is worship to him. Daily opportunities to live in a dependent relationship that brings mutual joy. The forever question swirling around in my mind: 'Why is independence our #1 goal?!' Avonlea encourages me to see the neediness and vulnerability of all of humanity and myself. We are needy people that cannot thrive in isolation and that is so, so good.

Jess and Alex are blessed. They are flourishing not only as they care for their daughter, but in declaring their own neediness and alternative good life as well.

If we want to become neighbors who are poor in spirit, we start with this kind of dependence on God's Spirit that we never outgrow, also known as prayer. We learn from Jesus and start talking to God more often. We ask him to change us from being emotionally detached and instead open our hearts to scary things like humility and sacrifice. We stay connected to the vine when we're at the mailbox, choosing grace rather than guilt. We don't rely on ourselves as good entertainers or conversationalists; we recognize our God as the better, most welcoming Host. Our stock is not in whether or not there's a pre-established sense of neighborhood community or thinking we can woo our neighbors with our own sort of street cred; rather we transfer our trust to the one who made the first neighborhood from scratch. All our fears, inadequacies, weaknesses, and limits make us needy for God. And in God's kingdom, the needier the better.

> Blessed are the poor in spirit, for theirs is the kingdom of heaven (Mt. 5:3)

God's Kingdom has Entered the Chat

We might wonder as we read the promises tagged to each beatitude—are these assurances for today or for tomorrow only? Does the promise that the poor in spirit will inherit God's kingdom only apply in eternity future or will we see it before then?

There's good news. In the words of New Testament scholar Scot McKnight: "This blessing, while its focus is future, begins now."[7]

But what does that mean? It's hard to imagine seeing the kingdom of heaven breaking into our now-neighborhoods. Heaven is the hope that anchors our soul and yet, at times, it can feel so far away.

Thankfully, we have a window into the experiences of Jesus' friends and followers, when they heard him say things like, "the kingdom of heaven is at hand" (Mt. 3:2, NASB) and "the kingdom of heaven has come near" (Mt. 4:17), all the while undoing the effects of sin's curse right before their very eyes. Everywhere he went—everywhere he stepped foot—the kingdom of God was imminent. God's future reign was no longer solely something to expect down the line. God's manifest presence was breaking in through the person of Jesus, bringing an overlap to our current and future realms.

This kingdom break in stopped and shocked onlookers when he un-withered the withered man's hand (Mk. 3:3–5), restored the sight of blind beggars like Bartimaeus (Mk. 10:46-52), and told the tongue of a deaf and mute man to "Be opened!" (Mk. 7:31–37). Curse-reversals such as these were signs that Jesus came not only to save, but to rule as king of a kingdom where his people would one day be healed and free forever.

Can you imagine what it was like for the woman who'd been hunched over for eighteen years to feel her back straighten as Jesus touched her with both hands (Lk. 13:11–13)? What about Malchus, the servant of the high priest who came to arrest Jesus (Lk. 22:50–51)? What ran through his mind after Jesus hooked his ear back on like it was no big thing? What happened when he went home that night? Did he sleep?!

Imagine the joy, surprise, laughter, and lightness that came to those who heard their stomachs growl and then sat with their jaws dropped as Jesus multiplied a few loaves and fish to satisfy the hunger of thousands, including their own. God's promised reign wasn't just for later; it was breaking through. His kingdom had entered the chat.

There will come a day when the kingdom will be fully here. Until that time, when we feebly live out these beatitude blueprints, we give our neighbors a taste of what's to come.

When Jesus said, "Blessed are the poor in spirit, for theirs is the kingdom of heaven," he was inviting us into abiding lives with these kinds of kingdom reversals. When we show up weak and needy for God's Spirit to move in our neighborhoods, we can imagine him using the smallest of steps to push back against the curse of culture wars and usher in cultures of hope and love. We wonder what kind of healing would come if we were to say hello or introduce ourselves to a next-door image-bearer. We imagine how he might interrupt our loneliness if our dinner tables were filled with neighborly conversations about our singleness, stress at work, or a difficult relationship with our teenager.

What joy and peace would it bring to the new refugee family who just moved in across the way if a group of neighbors reached out and welcomed them with open arms? How might God use that little phrase "Lord, help" to give us the words we need when a neighbor has lost their child … or the strength to stay in the moment and not offer words at all but rather the gift of our presence? Can you imagine how this kind of value-reversal might shift things on your street?

A Taste of the Kingdom

We are both low-level foodies. We try to be adventurous eaters, but we don't have the endless options of an urban neighborhood to indulge our ethnic food cravings. We began to rcalize however, that we do have neighbors from many different parts of the world in our own little neighborhood. As we pushed through language barriers and worked hard to learn names, friendships budded, and we had the idea for an international food sampling.

Then a reserved, Christ-following couple of Indian heritage—Arjun and Aadya—moved in from Chicago. Despite their insecurities that they weren't "leader-types" and their initial fears of it flopping, they got swept away by the idea. Arjun admitted this seemed like an answer to their daily prayers for God's help to love their neighbors well. They envisioned tables where neighbors could bring a large dish to share and small "exhibits," including recipes, artwork, herbs, spices, decorations, and flags. They loved the dream of gathering neighbors together to honor, esteem, and celebrate unique food flavors, skin colors, dialects, languages, and clothing. So, the vision of God's good image on display won them over and we prayed and we planned.

When the night finally arrived, neighbors from China, India, Israel, Brazil, Mexico, Bulgaria, and Turkey proudly presented their "Bite of the World," as Aadya called it. We had no idea there were so many cultures represented in our humble five-street neighborhood. The night felt magical, and we couldn't help but marvel at how God had used two people who'd been so tentative to do such important work—work like helping neighbors enjoy good food, shake hands, and properly pronounce each other's names.

We can't forget about Bina. Bina met Aadya in the planning process, and conversations about food led to deeper conversations about life and faith. Bina was recently divorced and her honor-shame culture had her wondering if the gods were angry with her. Aadya shared the hope of Christ and Bina asked her to pray to God on her behalf.

Arjun and Aadya reached out and received the blessing "theirs is the kingdom of heaven" when they showed up, poor in spirit, and took a step of faith. They offered Bina—and our whole neighborhood—a glimpse of the kingdom breaking into our little community.

Reimagining our neighborhoods begins with taking the first beatitude seriously. What would it look like to embrace the flourishing that comes with humility and dependence? And then to trust God's Spirit to continue the work that Jesus did in neighborhoods like Bethesda and Capernaum? Imagine him restoring in part now, what he will restore fully the day he returns: every square inch of our neighborhoods. Picture how he might lay hands on our gossip, jealousy, favoritism, and indifference, and cure these propensities within us. Can you visualize your neighbors being wooed by this alternative flourishing?

Envision yourself living in a community with neighbors marked by this contrasting humility, how it might serve as an up-close apologetic for our faith. Can you conceive how religious seekers and skeptics could be startled by this contradictory sort of posturing? What unexpected friendships might form with the family next door or the lady upstairs if rather than the same ol' self-absorption, they saw self-forgetfulness? Just think if our neighbors discovered the rest Jesus offers from the hustling, hiding, and striving that's demanded of them each day. What healing would come?

When we receive this first invitation to be poor in ourselves and rich in Christ, the kingdom of heaven breaks through. It comes as we begin to exchange our sweat for surrender and relax under his influence. Our vague notions of what heaven will be like are updated by the restorative work we see in our neighborhood corners. Jesus' reign and rule, which felt far off and distant, becomes our hope here and now. And prayerfully, as our own faith is strengthened, this upside-down flourishing will capture the attention and imagination of our neighbors, by instilling a sense of wonder that Jesus' kingdom is real after all.

For Reflection:

"Blessed are the poor in spirit, for theirs is the kingdom of heaven."

What might God want you to trust him for in your neighborhood?

Our daily prayer: "Lord, help!"

Neighbors and situations to pray for this week:

For Discussion:

1. Thinking about the introduction, how has your personal view of what it means to be "blessed" been shaped by the world's view of "the good life"? Contrast this with the biblical vision of flourishing. Are there points of overlap? Points of contrast?
2. Share whether you agree or disagree with this statement from the introduction: "We are not redeemed by the beatitudes, but the beatitudes show we've been redeemed." Explain your reasoning.
3. In one or two sentences, describe what it means to be poor in spirit.
4. Summarize the concept of the Me Monster and how it impacts the way we relate to our neighbors.
5. Choose one of the "nothing verses" and share how Jesus exhibited a "Lord, help" posture. How does this challenge you personally to increase your dependence on God?
6. List five to ten needs in your life that your neighbors could meet. What about being a "needy neighbor" challenges and/or energizes you?

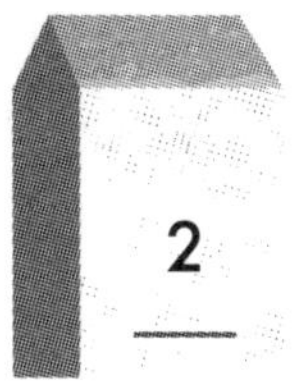

2

Good Grief

Jesus said: "Blessed are those who mourn, for they will be comforted."

The world says: "Blessed are those who numb out, for they will be comfortable."

When we were pregnant for the first time, we read a book called *What to Expect When You're Expecting*. It gave week-by-week development milestones, opinions on sleep and exercise, and thoughts on whether or not to eat fish and soft cheese. The book's widespread success resulted in a prequel and multiple sequels including what to expect the first year and the second year, a journal, and the baby-sitter's edition.

Thinking back to Jesus' first beatitude, perhaps some kind of subsequent spin-off would've been nice: *What to Expect When You're Poor in Spirit*. Once we acknowledge our neediness for God and choose dependence rather than self-reliance, what comes next? When we're poor in ourselves and rich in God, can we soon name and claim our fruitful Christian lives? Which week do we move from valley to victory?

> Blessed are those who mourn … (Mt. 5:4)

Gulp.

There were probably a range of responses among those seated on the grassy hill that day. If you'd been there listening to Jesus' second sermon point, perhaps you would have observed some sinking shoulders and heads in hands, or heard a quiet groan of frustration from the back of the crowd. Maybe some sat quietly processing while others wanted to boo or walk away. Whether government oppression, tough living conditions, class distinctions, or personal losses, these early disciples had already faced their fair share of suffering and it's plausible some had questions.

> *Blessed in mourning?! Is comfort the best I can hope for? What about fixing?*
> *Surely it's obvious all this negativity does not sell copies. Where is the health? Where is the wealth? When do we get to our best lives now?!*

Neighborhoods Not Right

After posting a picture on social media of a neighborhood gathering, a friend commented: "Wow, you guys have such a great community in your neighborhood. It's like you guys live in Disneyland."

Mmm, not quite.

Don't get us wrong, our neighbors are some of God's best gifts to us and we love them like family, but it's far from perfect over here. Despite the thousands of good things we could say about where we live, every neighborhood is filled with people, and people are filled with pain. No amount of either idealizing or demonizing certain contexts can change the fact that neighborhoods in city-centers, country outskirts, and everything in-between, all have their struggles.

Every place faces its particular challenges but there are universal ones, too. Image-bearers everywhere get unwanted doctor calls, experience financial tailspins, have annoying co-workers, and get lonely and depressed. In neighborhoods of all racial and socio-economic demographics, residents lose loved ones, fear rejection, long to be married or unmarried, and feel a loss of control when things don't go as planned. Every neighborhood is full of people who aren't sure how to resolve our conflicts, don't get enough sleep, and feel far from their families—even when they live close.

Whether the stressors are ones we bring home or they're already there, we're not always sure how to manage, or if we can. Rarely do people share with those around them how bad they're struggling.

Years ago, our next-door neighbor, Anne, was having out-patient surgery. We drove her to-and-from the hospital, checked on her in the afternoon, and then dropped off a meal so she didn't have to cook that evening. She couldn't believe it. "This might be normal in your church circles, but no one has ever made me a meal or done anything like this for me."

We met Ellen the day she moved in. On the outside, she was an attractive, middle-aged, single woman, from a small town who was actively engaged in child advocacy. We found out months later that she'd been eager to meet her neighbors because of her recent divorce and move from the only community she'd ever known. She feared being alone for the first time in her life.

Another neighbor, Teo, has shared about some tough mental health challenges. When he lost his job, he invited us to check in on him, even giving us a key to his house. There were some dark days where we weren't sure if he'd make it or not, and it grieved us to learn that we were his only friends.

It's been so long since we lost that first neighborhood, we can hardly remember what it was like. The memories have since faded and we all suffer from some grief fatigue.

The Ought Not

When we see the broken things in our neighborhoods, we can't help but think, "It shouldn't be this way." Our single neighbors shouldn't have to live in fear and isolation. Our elderly neighbors shouldn't be physically and mentally deteriorating from the effects of loneliness. Racism shouldn't divide our communities. Our neighborhoods shouldn't be characterized by high crime and senseless violence, with garbage here and there and broken car windows. Neither should they be characterized by disconnection, covetousness, self-indulgence, nor long-standing prejudices that demand sameness.

It ought not be this way.

Then again, why not? How *ought* our neighborhoods be? And who determines what they *ought* to be like?

Ought carries with it a sense of moral obligation to do that which is right. The very language of "ought" points to God's law and design. It implies a kind of righteous standard. There's something you ought to do, and something you ought *not* do.

There's a should and a should not. But where does this standard come from?

All oughts, ought nots, shoulds and should nots stem from Eden.

When confronted with the broken realities around them, even staunch atheists and relativists can't help themselves when they say things like, "Life isn't fair. It's not right. It shouldn't be this way." They betray their worldview with the language of ought because they're compelled to grieve the loss of the way things once were. We all miss that first neighborhood, the one with perfect peace and flourishing, where everything was as it ought to be.

The Bible calls this *shalom*, meaning prosperity and completeness.[1] Our taste of it was cut short, but we've never stopped dreaming of the day we'll have it again, for good. God's reign will be reestablished, and the needy will be protected. No more abuse, disordered eating or thinking, or satisfaction over others' failures. No more regret or heartache or blindness to our own faults. Imagine it: every neighborhood in the new creation steeped in security, justice, and joy.

Imagining life this way stirs hope, but confronting our current realities requires courage.

Sitting *Shiva*

Whether we know it or not, all of us have our own grief procedures. While grief is the internal experience of loss, mourning is its outward expression. Grief is what we feel and think; mourning is what we do. It includes the public rituals (funeral and burial procedures) and behaviors (wearing black) that declare this is not the way things were supposed to be. Mourning is our response to grief; it's how we show that we're shocked, angry, and sad.

The problem is, in the twenty-first-century West, we're often not very good at it.

Opening up our Bibles—particularly in the Old Testament—we discover a formal approach to mourning that facilitates the expression of one's sorrow. Though these Jewish customs might initially strike us as strange, God's people engaged in patterns of mourning which allowed for personal and corporate lament in beautifully structured ways. For example, when a loved one died, life went on hold, and time was set aside for mourning. This began with the initial days of intense bereavement which came to be called "sitting shiva."[2] *Shiva* is the Hebrew word for seven, and refers to the seven days following the burial which were designated for weeping (Gen. 23:2) and lamentation (2 Sam. 1:17). This was followed by further time for expressions of grief, lasting thirty days out from the burial. Setting aside time to mourn was one way to give permission to the bereaved that it was okay to not be okay.

In ancient Near Eastern culture, mourning was dramatic. Today, if we're looking for healthy ways to express what's inside, our friends may suggest activities such as journaling or painting. While these are incredibly helpful exercises, they're also very ... *quiet*. Prophets like Ezekiel and Joel however, emphasized weeping, wailing, and groaning in anguish (Ezek. 27:31; Joel 1:5) because grief is sometimes loud.

Sometimes when we're torn apart on the inside, we want to show it on the outside. Tearing one's robe was an outward way to express the internal rupture that was happening, to say: *I'm destroyed. I'm undone.* Job was so beside himself when he got the news that a desert storm had stolen the lives of his kids that he shaved his head (Job 1:20). Mordecai and Esther wouldn't eat when they heard of Haman's plans to destroy God's people (Est. 4:3,16). The Ninevites were so remorseful over their sins, they all put on a coarse, goat-hair garment called sackcloth (along with all their animals!) in the hope God would have mercy on them (Jon. 3:8–9). After being sexually abused and assaulted by her half-brother, Tamar covered her head in ashes (2 Sam. 13:19). These simple rituals served as their picket signs toward sin and death.

For ancient Israelites, practices such as tearing clothes, weeping, wailing, and wearing sackcloth and ashes were built into their culture of grief. For us moderns, we will mourn in our own unique ways according to our beliefs, cultures, and temperaments. Nonetheless, those of us who consider ourselves private, internal processors or are bent toward a silver lining might do well in asking: *What can we learn from our Jewish ancestors and the structured, expressive nature of their mourning? How can I bring what's on the inside to the outside?*

Allergic to Grief

Runny nose, itchy, watery eyes, hives, and swelling are among symptoms that our body may present when having an allergic reaction. This happens when a foreign organism such as bacteria or viruses are found within the body and our defenses go up. Our immune system sends protective antibody armies to confront the pollen, eggs, milk, or mold. Based on their intolerant nature, and borrowing from Star Wars, we could fittingly nickname these physical troops "The Resistance."

Sometimes our bodies fight against the very medicines we take to heal ourselves. This happened a few weeks ago when I (Elizabeth) insisted to my doctor that I wasn't allergic to

Penicillin (even though the records said I was). Ten days later, I was covered in polka dots … and humiliation.

In a similar way, we're allergic to grief. When we experience loss, it's like a foreign presence is introduced to our system, sirens are sounded and a quintillion warriors are there yelling, "Noooooo" in protest. Grief takes place inside the body and—try as we may to make it go away—this inner war affects our thoughts and feels. Our bodies keep score of these internal traumas, and we feel heartsick and weary because we were never designed to function in a broken world.

Grief can show up in our feelings of fear, loneliness, and confusion. We might feel guilty or withdrawn and wonder if we'll ever be happy again. It's unpredictable and relentless. It can be indirect, paralyzing, and easily triggered.

When we mourn, we let what's on the inside come to the outside. We, too, cry "Noooo!" and say out loud that we're not okay. It's our public display of resistance that it's not just another Tuesday and we won't go on with business as usual. Rather than bottling, denying, or pretending, mourning is an act of acknowledgment that our suffering is real, and that the world isn't as it ought to be.

In this second beatitude, Jesus is speaking into one of our biggest questions, our problem of pain. Jesus didn't see suffering as an illusion as some philosophies do, nor consider hope something to deaden ourselves toward or overcome. He doesn't want us to be snuffed out in a non-self state. Rather than deny our suffering, he invites us right into it and promises flourishing. He beckons to us from an elevator headed to a dreaded lower level of mourning, a place we both fear and resist.

Can we trust him?

Pain, our Unifying Link

We all have our fixes. These are the things that temporarily numb us out and take the edge off. Netflix, drive-throughs, retail therapy, pain pills, sleep, ice cream, work … We long to disassociate from the hard things in our lives, even if it's for thirty minutes. In the words of Bob Wiley, we want a "vacation from our problems."[3]

The truth is, we've believed a counterfeit beatitude: Blessed are those who numb out, for they will be comfortable.

Jesus begs to differ.

All around us, neighbors are suffering from alcoholism, self-doubt, and chronic illnesses. The man across the street might be dealing with crippling anxiety, insomnia, and lack of purpose. The mother a few doors up may be crying herself to sleep each night desperately worried about how to make ends meet, and the children who walk past every morning dreading the bully at school. Do we wince? Do we cry out to God? Do we mourn? Does their pain impact us, too?

One street over, Callie—one of the most winsome and witty neighbors we know—received a serious, life-changing health diagnosis. Multiple neighbors down our street have struggled with unbearable infertility journeys while two other families we know have faced unexpected pregnancies later in life. We've seen neighbors lose their marriages and watched as the Clarkes and the Cookes went from being the best of friends to barely speaking with one another. Neighbors can feel despairing, depressed, and isolated.

We may not be connected in Christ, but pain can connect us in another way. How might this unifying link of pain impact our capacity to love our neighbors, even those with whom we feel we have nothing in common? Have our own struggles with estrangement, addictions, and dysphoria informed the ways in which we might respond to someone experiencing the same thing, but without God's Word and his Spirit?

God's prophets sometimes stepped in as these pain receptors, sounding the sirens with messages that God's people were not okay. Jeremiah felt it deep: "Since my people are crushed, I am crushed" (Jer. 8:21). Micah wept: "Because of this, I will weep and wail; I will go about barefoot and naked. I will howl like a jackal and moan like an owl" (Mic. 1:8).

But what if we don't feel this way? I (Chris) am not the most empathetic guy. I love my comfort and I already feel maxed by my own junk—and my family's junk. The thought of attuning more to other peoples' problems kinda gives me hives. It's overwhelming and I don't have the energy for it. If I'm honest, I'd rather tune out than tune in.

If you find you have a lack of sensitivity to pain and your messaging system is somewhat broken, you're in good company. When this happens to our bodies, doctors perform a type of decompression surgery on the spine which reverses numbness, and the pain is often immediate! Spiritually speaking, this kind of operation happens on our hearts too. As Jesus comes to us comfort-seekers, he offers a new kind of flourishing wrapped up in his gift of pain. The good news is that his true comfort will follow.

> I will give you a new heart and put a new spirit in you; I will remove from you your heart of stone and give you a heart of flesh (Ez. 36:26).

Not Just in Theory

Having previously recovered from thyroid cancer, in May 2020, pastor and theologian Tim Keller was diagnosed with stage IV terminal pancreatic cancer. After his diagnosis and before his death, he shared how suffering shifts our perspective:

> What's happened with the cancer is suddenly we say I can't make heaven out of this earth because it's going to be taken away from us. And it just jolts you so much that you have to say I'm going to make heaven my heaven and God my heaven. And here is what is really weird—when you actually make heaven your heaven, the joys of the earth are more poignant than they used to be. That's what is so strange. We enjoy our day more than we ever did.[4]

Jesus let earth be earth and heaven be heaven. He knew this world was not as it ought to be and didn't mince words. Rather than promise us honey and money here, he guaranteed a temporary heartache saying, "In this world you will have trouble. But take heart! I have overcome the world" (Jn. 16:33). Peter picked up on this and tried to set low expectations for his readers: "Dear friends, do not be surprised at the fiery ordeal that has come on you to test you, as though something strange were happening to you" (1 Pet. 4:12). Anyone offering lasting peace now is selling a lie.

Jesus also knew our pain wasn't pretend. He didn't come explaining our suffering away as a social construct or something we can rise above. No, he came as a "man of suffering, and familiar with pain" (Is. 53:3). But he also didn't check out, numb out, or want to be "snuffed out" into a state of non-existence.

He stayed present and made himself vulnerable by loving and losing. When his best friend died, he cried (Jn. 11:35). When he approached Jerusalem and thought about the spiritual ruin and impending desolation of his city, he wept (Lk. 19:41). When he was overcome with anguish in the garden, he sweated drops of blood and prayed: "Father, if you are willing, take this cup from me; yet not my will, but yours be done" (Lk. 22:42). And the author of Hebrews tells us: "During the days of Jesus' life on earth, he offered up prayers and petitions with fervent cries and tears to the one who could save him from death" (Heb. 5:7). He wasn't afraid to cry.

He didn't come with some hypothetical theory for responding to our bad news; he lived what we're up against. This means he's not aloof or indifferent to the stresses and messes in our lives and, crucially, in our neighbors' lives. How can we know this? Because he expressed on the outside what was on the inside, mourning both tenderly and fiercely.

Jesus modeled good grief for us and didn't stop there. When he faced the curse of sin and death and felt its devastating effects, he tore more than his robe—he tore his own body. On the cross, Jesus cried out in a loud voice, and in that moment, "the curtain of the temple was torn in two from top to bottom" (Mt. 27:51). When Jesus' body broke, so did the barrier between us and God. His willingness to mourn brought us the opportunity for eternal flourishing, the ultimate gift of his pain.

He let earth be earth, but he also let heaven be heaven. He gave us a peek into the heavenly realms in the book of Revelation: "'He will wipe every tear from their eyes. There will be no more death' or mourning or crying or pain, for the old order of things has passed away" (Rev. 21:4).

He says, "I've been there, you're not alone, and hope is coming." This is what we can offer our neighbors when we believe the second beatitude, when we go against all our intuition and believe God that flourishing will come to those who mourn. Suffering doesn't have to be the end of their story.

Neighborhoods Soothed

Years ago, a movie came out called *Bruce Almighty*. After complaining that he could do God's job better than he does, Morgan Freeman's God-character comes to offer Bruce the position. But when Bruce is given supernatural powers to hear peoples' prayers, he soon discovers he just can't take it. His mind fills with the noise of a million needs and it's all too much. It overwhelms him, he's not built for it, and he becomes desperate to give the job back to God. Even with some superhuman power-up's, Bruce realizes that he's limited in his capacity to handle the scope of others' needs.

Maybe there's a part of us that fears the more we engage with our neighbors, the more it could all take over our lives. Maybe we stay distant because we know we're barely surviving as it is. Doesn't God know we're limited human beings? How much can we handle? Empathy seems too tall an order.

God knows our limits better than we do. He's not asking us to show up at our neighbors' houses with all the reserves and all the answers doing what only he can do. Instead, he invites us tired and weary mourners to sit down and dine at his table. Comfort and compassion are on the menu and our neighbors are invited, too.

This won't be the last time Jesus will promise comfort. Before he heads home, he announces to his disciples that the

Holy Spirit will soon be coming and will be present with them as their Comforter. The word he uses is often translated as "Helper," "Counselor," or "Advocate." Jesus did not leave his friends alone in their losses and ought nots and sad feelings. He did not say, "I will check back in on you" or "Good luck navigating all this" or "You'll be fine." He knows without him, we won't be.

We can't do this life alone, we need him right there with us at every moment and from the beginning, that's where he promised he'd be: "The Lord himself goes before you and will be with you; he will never leave you nor forsake you" (Deut. 31:8). This isn't something he says once. He says it again and again and again: *I will be with you.*

God cannot go against his own nature as our ever-present Comforter. He is truth, he cannot lie. He is eternal, he cannot be finite. He is good, he cannot do evil ... He is the "God of all comfort" (2 Cor. 1:3), he cannot stay away from us or be cool and indifferent toward his children. When we are in distress, he doesn't plug his ears or ignore us. His arms are outstretched, ready to soothe. It's who he is, our consoling, compassionate God. With his comfort, he says: *I'm right here. I've got you. I'm not going anywhere.*

> Can a mother forget the baby at her breast and have no compassion on the child she has borne? Though she may forget, I will not forget you! (Is. 49:15).

> As a father has compassion on his children, so the Lord has compassion on those who fear him (Ps. 103:13).

> The Lord, the Lord, the compassionate and gracious God, slow to anger, abounding in love and faithfulness (Ex. 34:6).

What would change in our neighborhoods if we were changed by the comfort of God? If rather than "grieve like the rest of mankind, who have no hope" (1 Thes. 4:13), we had a light at the end of the tunnel?

Imagine if as believers, we mourned by fasting from food rather than God when things weren't going right. What if we didn't go numb but experienced the soothing power of God's presence in the thick of our pain and fears? How would our mindset shift?

Our friends Owen and Siobhan, despite living alongside long-term residents with minimal turnover, told us they felt sad that "their neighborhood didn't feel like a neighborhood." Steeped in a culture of independence, it didn't help that their little row of houses had no sidewalks or streetlights, making it all the more challenging to connect. The fact that neighbors were disconnected and unseen—both literally and figuratively—didn't sit right with them. They determined that their lack of lighting wouldn't have the last word and have brought God's comfort by building a vibrant community through prayer and soup nights.

Or maybe like Kelly, we'd realize it's not right that many of our neighbors suffer from touch starvation, many of them going long stretches without any human contact. With increased digitalization and more people working from home, our neighbors—and ourselves—have less and less physical contact. Rather than overcorrecting our culture's abuse and misuse of touch, we'd wisely and intentionally extend God's comfort through small, physical interactions that are safe, godly and appropriate. For a neighbor who hasn't had physical contact for months, a hug, handshake or even a friendly pat on the back can showcase God's comfort in a major way.[5]

Looking out our windows, we'd be aware that we're surrounded by image-bearers who feel exhausted, invisible, and heartsick. We'd be slower to judge and assume the worst, and quicker to pray these words with Paul:

> Praise be to the God and Father of our Lord Jesus Christ, the Father of compassion and the God of all comfort, who comforts us in all our troubles, so that we can comfort those in any trouble with the comfort we ourselves receive from God (2 Cor. 1:3–4).

This is how our neighbors will know the God of all comfort, the One who is not far from them, who wants to use the bad for their good and give them eternal rest: when the comfort God has shown us on the inside shows up on the outside … when the comforted become the comforters, when the soothed become the soothers. When we say to our neighbors: "I've been there, I am with you. Here is the love Jesus has shown me—he is the true binder of broken hearts."

For Reflection:

"Blessed are those who mourn, for they will be comforted."

What emotions are stirred in you as you engage with Jesus' invitation to mourn the brokenness in your neighborhood?

Our daily prayer: "Lord, help me to mourn the sad things around me, to know your comfort, and to offer it to my neighbors, too."

Neighbors and situations to pray for this week:

For Discussion:

1. If you could change one wrong in your neighborhood, what would it be and why?
2. Define mourning. How is Jesus' invitation into mourning different from other cultural approaches to pain (numbing out, avoidance, denial, etc.)? Why is it so difficult?
3. What impact does it have on you to think about the ways in which Jesus mourned? How does his reaction convict and/or move you?
4. Name a time when you experienced Christ's comfort while mourning. How could you envision extending this kind of comfort to your neighbors in their pain?
5. A prayer of lament is one way to mourn (outwardly express one's inner grief). Use these categories to form your own prayer of lament for your neighborhood:

   Complaint (naming specific ways you see brokenness in your neighborhood)
   Reflection on God's character (for example, remembering God's love, faithfulness, nearness, and so on)
   Petition (asking for God's intervention, comfort, healing, and help)

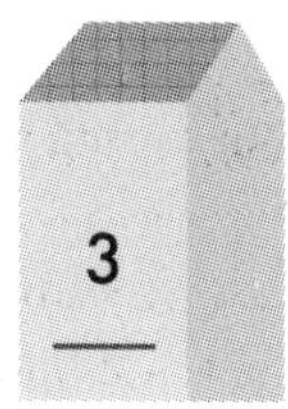

From Me-ness to Meekness

Jesus said: "Blessed are the meek, for they will inherit the earth."

The world says: "Blessed are those who consider their own wants first, for they will manifest their best lives now."

Several years ago, members of our HomeOwners Association decided we were due for some new signage. Coincidentally, the bigger, more expensive neighborhood across the street had just installed their name in triumphant rod-iron lettering against a gorgeous stone backdrop with landscaping and a water feature. We feared our smaller pocketbooks might lead to some neighborhood conflict, and we were right.

At every opportunity something could go south, it did. From the outset, there was disagreement regarding the overall design and bickering over its precise placement. Further along in the process, neighbors were angry regarding money management and feared we'd overextended ourselves. Neighbors used social media as a forum to express thoughts and concerns, but it felt confrontational and impersonal. Several felt attacked, disrespected, and underappreciated. Others felt misled. Opinions were dismissed and shots were fired. Rather than seek to understand, most sought to be understood. One neighbor told us he was overwhelmed by all the negativity and contemplating a move.

In situations like these, we just wish everyone around us would get on and do things the right way—*our* way.

But Jesus has a different agenda:

> Blessed are the meek, for they will inherit the earth (Mt. 5:5).

Meekness?!

Meekness is traditionally put in the corner. It gets the shaft when it's conveniently advertised as self-doubt and insecurity. Often meekness sounds more like code for timidity and passivity, and if we were to guess, it probably pairs well with lots of words beginning with "un"—uninspiring, unattractive, unambitious. "You mean blessed are the boring?" we nervously joke, shifting our weight from foot to foot.

This can't be the roadmap for how Jesus' followers participate in seeing his kingdom come, can it? His original hearers were enduring brutal force under Roman occupation and hoping for a big swing of the power pendulum in their direction. With Jesus' arrival and this speech, there were expectations for some needed wins: no more forced submission to the wrong king, no more being under someone else's thumb. A chat about voluntary submission doesn't quite scratch the itch.

Our intuition tells us meekness is for the people who won't and can't, those who are fearful, indecisive, or apathetic. When the whistle blows and push comes to shove, we need leaders with charisma, we need movers and shakers. We need to get things done. If we're ever to turn things around spiritually in our neighborhoods, we're going to need some kind of wow-factor to woo people to Jesus ... aren't we? Meekness sounds like loser language.

Trust = None

A few years ago, I (Elizabeth) ran into Gloria when we were both out walking our dogs. We'd seen each other around and our kids had played together a few times. Although not close, we had good rapport. As we walked the dogs that day, our small talk progressed into a deeper conversation about her faith journey. She was raised in the church but felt rejected by her community when she left her husband for another woman. She shared her story, her hurts, and her heart. What was she looking for in that first deep conversation with me? Objection? Correction? Direction? Maybe meekness.

Of course, it's not just Gloria. Confidence in organized religion has hit an all-time low. The unveiling of power dynamics and scandals amongst priests and pastors with culpable support staff has been a turn-off. The biblical sexual ethic feels outdated and restrictive to outsiders and news stories make some doubt if they'd want to fit in Christian circles, even if they could. Some feel Christian ethics are an oxymoron.

Given these realities, the overall decline of church attendance, the rise of those who identify as religious nones[1], and the ever-growing politicization of evangelicalism, we need a "step back committee." It's a team of people who will "step back" and help consider the blind spots and potential pitfalls of something. We formed a step back committee when we were naming our first child—be it possible misspellings, nicknames, mispronunciations—we wanted a team who would be completely honest with us.

We need a step back committee when it comes to the messaging of our faith.

The truth is, our spiritually unaffiliated neighbors aren't only staying home on Sunday mornings because they don't like institutions. It's not just the church out there they don't trust, it's the church right here. At home, next door. It's you and me. At times, they feel we've lacked the ability—and desire—to find common ground and work together. They see us choose emotional distance when our flags are different because we feel we have to do what's best for our families. They see us weigh the cost-benefit for whether to engage, serve, and be present … and conclude that the work just isn't worth it. We're suspicious of our neighbors, so we just hang out with virtual strangers in our social media feeds because we feel safer and think we can turn that off whenever we want to.

It's hard to be honest, but we have to ask: Can our next-door neighborhood nones see a brand of Christianity they want to try on? Or do they look at us and see lives left wanting?

Poor in Spirit Remix

We love a good throwback. When a top chef gives an updated nod to a classic dish, or a sports team wears a color that's reminiscent of a previous era, or—as of late—when our oldest daughter uses her iPad to create an interesting remix of a current hit song, we feel nostalgic about the original, but appreciate the twist.

When Jesus said, "Blessed are the meek, for they will inherit the earth," it was a throwback to the first beatitude. While being poor in spirit has to do with our ongoing neediness in our vertical relationship with God, meekness is the outward expression of that humble posture in our horizontal relationship with others. It's a remix of Jesus' previous invitation away from self-importance, and shown through service. They're like two temperature checks—one internal, one external. When we're poor in spirit, it shows up in meekness.

Far from inaction, meekness is the gentle courage to consider others as more important than ourselves. It is the selfless act of submitting to someone else's needs and wants. Meekness requires the strength to temper our own agenda with a compassionate consideration for our neighbor's perspective. This self-control is directed by care and concern and voluntarily bends when needed. It is patient, it is yielding, it is pleasant. It is fine with second place.

When we are poor in spirit, meekness is what our neighbors see. It's the first beatitude made visible. How do our neighbors know we've rejected our self-sufficient Me Monsters and are God-dependent? We're dressed in meekness. It's our jersey, our team uniform. Those who are poor in spirit present as meek.

> Therefore, as God's chosen people, holy and dearly loved, clothe yourselves with compassion, kindness, humility, gentleness [meekness] and patience (Col. 3:12).

This outward-facing trait is kind of like Pilates—it looks easy until you do it. Some of us have watched as our instructors have eased flawlessly into the Jackknife or Snake and Twist Position and then naively pulled out our own mat to try it ourselves (*if you know, you know).* Pilates requires core strength, stability, flexibility, and endurance. Similarly, meekness is an exercise in strength and control and as we practice it, we realize we're pretty squishy without it.

We have examples of this in Scripture. Moses, after forty years of bearing with the whines and complaints of God's people, was referred to as the meekest man of his day (Num. 12:3). David demonstrated meekness toward King Saul—the man who madly sought his life—when he chose deference rather than vengeance on multiple occasions. This "I am second" mentality filled him with the compassion to mourn when he learned of Saul's death, though it brought with it relief surrounding his own safety and the long-awaited fulfillment of his own rise to power. Following these acts of submission and soft-heartedness came his commitment to honor Saul's life by adopting his disabled grandson Mephibosheth, giving him a seat of honor at his table. Then we have Ruth, who made herself vulnerable through fierce loyalty to her mother-in-law Naomi when, as a widowed immigrant, she bet on a better future through meekness.

These stories of meekness may or may not have felt so noteworthy at the time. These were real sacrifices each made in their everyday lives to relinquish their rights for the sake of loving God and others. And this is where the curveball really comes. It's when we realize this underrated virtue we shrugged off as "meh-ness" threatens our chance to kick up our feet and rest now. Friends, meekness is a death sentence. Make that plural. It's the continuous call for us to love our neighbors as ourselves by dying to our viewpoints, programs, and timetables.

> For whoever wants to save their life will lose it, but whoever loses their life for me will find it (Mt. 16:25).

> … the Son of Man did not come to be served, but to serve, and to give his life as a ransom for many (Mt. 20:28).

In our neighborhoods, these death sentences can be surprisingly ordinary. We want to love our neighbors in a broad and theological sense, but not always in a way that impacts us at home. Do we feel put out, or gladly make the extra effort required to coordinate a wrongly delivered package? Being good neighbors is nice if kept vague, but can we freely agree to helping with a neighbor's pet on the weekend or remain generous toward the neighborhood kids who nearly empty our pantry? What about patiently enduring the untimely use of a leaf blower? How much do these disturbances disturb us?

These commonplace occurrences can expose our egos and privileged perspectives and require us to revisit our first two beatitudes. Rather than self-justifying these reflexes, perhaps we should pause and grieve our meekless-ness.

Meekness or Manifesting

Recently, we streamed the first episode of *WeCrashed* on Apple TV+, the true story of the rise and fall of the billion-dollar company, WeWork.[2] Anne Hathaway and Jared Leto play the two scrappy entrepreneurs who share the hope of getting rich quick. Hathaway's character, Rebekah, starts out as a Zen yoga instructor who believes she can create and attract a better life. "I manifested you," she tells Adam. "It's true. I did. It works. If you put positive vibes out into the world, the universe will open doors ... Focus on your spiritual energy, emanating those vibrations." With her eyes closed, while she's still speaking, a wealthy investor is ringing their phone.

Manifestation is strongly rooted in the New Age spirituality movement but has become widely popularized by mainstream voices. It's the idea that we can align ourselves and our energy with the universe and—through the law of attraction—draw good things our way. We can think, speak, and feel our intentions into realities. You want love? Success? A new car? Well with the #369method, all you do is write down your request from the universe three times in the morning, six times in the afternoon, and nine times at night for 33 days, or 45 to be safe. Call it and it will come. Long story short, you are your own personal genie, capable of giving yourself the happily-ever-after you've always dreamed of.[3]

If you've been around Christianity for some time now, this might ring a bell and sound oddly familiar to you. It's a secular version of prosperity theology, also known as the prosperity gospel. It's the idea that with enough faith, we can name and claim all the health, wealth, and happiness we could ever want. This ideology became a crowd-pleaser in the United States post-World War II with its appeal to those struggling to make ends meet, but quickly spread like crazy to Latin America, Asia, and Africa.[4]

Prosperity theology and New Age philosophies can have a lot in common. Both call for collaboration with a higher power—either with God or with the universe. Both affirm some kind of divine self-empowerment where fate lies in our own hands, and we determine our futures. Faith and gratitude are pledged in exchange for capital gains and doubt is a big "no-no." Both give us the counterfeit beatitude which says: *Blessed are those who consider their own wants first, for they will manifest their best lives now.*

Our beliefs about these things affect the ways in which we show up as neighbors. A habit of manifesting our destinies three times in the morning, six times in the afternoon, and nine times at night—whether literally or figuratively—crowds out the margin to consider others. The prosperity gospel tells me I deserve good things, not that I should put these on hold to help out someone else. When we're steeped in a culture of snatching what we believe is rightfully ours, neighboring feels outside the box.

Why listen and try to understand while your neighbor goes off on a rant about something that doesn't pertain to you? Why clean up messes that aren't yours or quietly contribute toward the overall welfare of your neighborhood? Why spend time planning a small gathering for those you hardly know? Why keep investing in a relationship with someone who's lost spiritual interest or whose faith has been dismantled and is now critical of the church you love?

Jesus has a different way of doing things. Meekness tells us the truth—life isn't all about us.

Where manifesting turns us inward, meekness turns us outward. Our newsfeeds aren't trending stories about manifesting lowly, ordinary lives of longsuffering rootedness. People aren't going viral on TikTok for naming and claiming attitudes of sacrificial faithfulness. Yet, meekness has a message worth sharing.

Undercover Boss

When Larry O'Donnell was president and COO of Waste Management, one of the world's largest trash and recycling companies, he decided to go undercover. At that point, he had a $13 billion business with 45,000 employees and he wanted a look behind the scenes. So, he "traded his executive office and expense account for a hard hat and bagged lunch" and posed as a new recruit. He toured the landfills, picking up trash and cleaning out porta potties.[5]

Upon revealing his identity, he surprised his employees by rewarding their hard work he had observed while under wraps. They were shocked that their president would go to the trouble of walking in their shoes. He knew their struggles because his back had hurt, too. They had seen him become like one of them, dressing like them and doing the same dirty work. They couldn't believe he would stoop so low.

Jesus also stooped low and in doing so, he showed a strength the Greek polytheists of his day had never seen. They'd seen gods of war, gods of wrath, and gods of wisdom; they'd never seen a God condescend with humility.

He came to our level. The God of the universe took on flesh and became like one of us. He left privilege for an uphill battle, experiencing the same things that were hard for us. He traded a million comforts for a million problems—problems he considered priceless, like you and me. He wasn't manifesting $10,000 or power from the universe, he was trusting his Father to meet his needs while he loved his neighbors sacrificially.

Jesus was meek and wasn't embarrassed to describe himself this way saying, "Come to me, all who labor and are heavy laden, and I will give you rest. Take my yoke upon you, and learn from me, for I am gentle [meek[6]] and lowly in heart, and you will find rest for your souls" (Mt. 11:28–29, ESV).

Dane Ortlund points out that meekness is at the very heart of who God is:

> [The Bible] startles us with [a God] whose infinitude of perfections is matched by His infinitude of gentleness. Indeed, His perfections include His perfect gentleness. It is who He is. It is His very heart. Jesus Himself said so.[7]

Jesus was the perfect picture of God's meekness and Paul knew imitating this meek mindset was our pathway to relational flourishing: "... in humility value others above yourselves, not looking to your own interests but each of you to the interests of the others. In your relationships with one another, *have the same mindset as Christ Jesus*" (Phil. 2:3–5, emphasis added).

Jesus demonstrated this in his life and in his death. Thankfully, he doesn't quit on self-focused sinners and navel-gazers. He came for the easily offended and those who easily offend. He gave his time away to those with narcissistic tendencies and opened his arms to meekness-avoiders. There's even forgiveness when our good goals slide into self-focused manifesting.

Knowing that the God of the universe would condescend with such meekness has the potential to startle us in such a way that it just might persuade us this is truly the best way to live as neighbors.

Prosperity Theology Revised

John shows another picture of a meek Messiah down on his knees, bending before his friends in servitude:

> Jesus knew that the Father had put all things under his power, and that he had come from God and was returning to God; *so* he got up from the meal, took off his outer clothing, and wrapped a towel around his waist. After that, he poured water into a basin and began to wash his disciples' feet, drying them

> with the towel that was wrapped around him (Jn. 13:3–5, emphasis added).

Notice the little word "so." Jesus "knew that the Father had put all things under his power"; he knew "that he had come from God and was returning to God" … *so* he got up to serve. He knew where he'd come from and where he was going. He knew good things were coming and that this life wasn't forever.

He knew the promise, "the meek will inherit the earth."

For those sitting on the grassy hill, this earth inheritance wasn't a new topic. They were hearing "promised land" language, which meant property, but it also meant prosperity. When Jesus mentions their earth inheritance, their minds would have gone to Old Testament passages describing "a land with large, flourishing cities … houses filled with all kinds of good things … wells … vineyards and olive groves …" where they would "eat and [be] satisfied" (Deut. 6:10–11). It's the happily-ever-after—all that we've lost and all that we've mourned, restored. All we've missed out on, we'll have. Our labor will be without frustration, our relationships will be healed, our sleep will be peaceful, and sin will no longer have a place.

Jesus could get down and wash his neighbors' feet because he had the big picture in mind, just like Moses who, "chose to be mistreated along with the people of God rather than to enjoy the fleeting pleasures of sin. He regarded disgrace for the sake of Christ as of greater value than the treasures of Egypt, because he was looking ahead to his reward" (Heb. 11:25–26).

Think about all the little death sentences Jesus had in conversations when people spoke over him, told him what to do, misunderstood him, and hurried him along. He served his neighbors in little ways, big ways, and then all the way. He never held back, laying down his life, not only emblematically, but literally dying once and for all, saying, "Greater love has no one than this: to lay down one's life for one's friends" (Jn. 15:13).

With foot-washing and death sentences, Jesus changed the narrative. While our cultures and intuitions tell us to chase the perks, follow our hearts, and "do what makes us happy," Jesus shows us a different kind of prosperity theology, one that waits. One that dies to the passing pleasure of "now," and lives for a future inheritance.

Making Margin

One of the most beloved (and meek) neighbors of all time was Fred Rogers, mastermind producer, musician, puppeteer, and host of the children's educational series, *Mister Rogers' Neighborhood*. After attending Pittsburgh Theological Seminary, he was ordained in 1963 as a Presbyterian evangelist for television, believing the space he was creating for himself and children to be sacred.[8] Rev. George Wirth, his pastor and friend, described the spiritual nature of his work. He noted that while many ministers wore a collar, Rogers wore a sweater. And while others preached oratorical sermons, Mr. Rogers' preaching came in his gentle way of seeing right into children's hearts.

Fred Rogers' approach to reach children was radical in many ways, including his use of time and silence. A child development advisor, who worked closely with Rogers behind the scenes, commented on how he delighted in the quiet spaces, describing an instance in which he showed children how long a minute lasts by holding out an egg timer and waiting silently until sixty seconds had passed. Other actors noted that though the time passed slowly, none was wasted.

When he was honored with the Lifetime Achievement Award at the 1997 Emmys, he deflected the attention of the accolade by asking the celebrity audience to take ten seconds of silence with him to honor the memory of those who had cared deeply for them and wanted their best. As the room went quiet, some broke out in an uncomfortable burst of laughter. But then, as those ten seconds of silence went on, the camera panned to actors wiping tears as they thought of the helpers who'd made a difference in their lives.

Like a teacher who quiets their voice to command their students' attention, Mr. Rogers' unhurried posture stopped and captured hearts. The simple way he used margin to make room for others in conversation showed that meekness can indeed be captivating.

We can do this, too. Instead of pushing up against the clock, we can leave a few minutes early for our meeting in hopes we'll have the chance to run into a neighbor. Rather than rushing, we'll find we're able to pause and be present and curious in the conversation. Building in this kind of breathing room to consider others is strangely relaxing.

We can make margin in our budgets as well. In lieu of assigning every penny to our standard self-categories, we can choose to set aside some extra for those living around us who are going through hard or unexpected circumstances, like the loss of a pet or a stressful season at work. There's joy in making wiggle room with our funds to give someone a gift card or provide some extra meals or splurge on some flowers for a neighbor who could use some encouragement. When possible, these kinds of reserves foster joy from left field.

This idea goes way back. In ancient Israel, God had woven the idea of margin into Israel's laws and by-laws so that the neighbors would take notice. Think about the law of gleaning:

> When you reap the harvest of your land, do not reap to the very edges of your field or gather the gleanings of your harvest. Do not go over your vineyard a second time or pick up the grapes that have fallen. Leave them for the poor and the foreigner. I am the LORD your God (Lev. 19:9–10).

God wanted his people to leave some margin for their vulnerable neighbors because it reflected that he valued the vulnerable. Moses knew that righteous acts like these would stand out to the neighbors whose gods were inequitable and stingy, asking, "what other nation is so great as to have such righteous decrees and laws as this body of laws I am setting before you today?" (Deut. 4:8).

Meekness makes room.

Going Second

Just imagine if we lived this way in our neighborhoods, if the Spirit slowed us down and supplied us with the courage to love our neighbors as ourselves. What if rather than hope and wait for them to come to our churches, we gave our next-door nones a taste of this gentle service? What would adjust in our schedules and social media posts?

How would meekness change the tiny interactions we have with neighbors we hardly know? Imagine the contrast if, instead of making judgments from afar or assuming they're just fine, Christ's lowliness helped us enter their worlds. Meekness could slow us down enough to know if they needed a meal, an outdoor tool of some sort, or a word of encouragement. And it would give us the humility to receive the same from them.

Think about if—rather than the stench of entitlement and self-preoccupation—we carried the refreshing aroma of Christ's meekness and looked not only to our own interest, but to the interests of our neighbors. What if they heard us talk about our bonuses and vacation packages as gifts rather than gods? Would it challenge their thoughts on what's worth living for or cause them to consider a different kind of prosperity theology, one where the meek inherit the earth? Imagine the joy of seeing irreligious neighbors softened by this unpretentious posture as they observe believing neighbors serving in their communities. Picture how it might puzzle the religiously burnt-out to see believing neighbors be the first to volunteer to help maintain common areas, serve in thankless roles on a neighborhood board, or continue to serve tirelessly at events for years and years?

How would conversations shift? What if seeing meekness as a God-empowered virtue were to increase our ability to empathize and diffuse tense situations with neighbors when discussing neighborhood issues (like neighborhood signs, hypothetically speaking)? What if instead of demanding and defending our thoughts and perspectives, they got to see us express our convictions with a willingness to learn?

Imagine the walls that would come down if, in our neighborly chats, we slowed down enough to really hear them, if we valued quiet instead of immediately piling in with our own opinions, relying on God's strength to defer. How would it impact them to see someone who doesn't need to rush or be first to get all their words in because there is a delayed inheritance coming? Envision the unity and reconciliation that could come to our neighborhoods if we asked God for help here. Imagine the allure of seeing God's people submit in love where there is difference. With a front row to this beatitude, can't you picture how some might consider the beauty of a God who regards the inherent worth and human dignity of all?

Just imagine if we passed on treasure and pleasure now, and placed greater value in our neighbors knowing Jesus. God wants this for us. Our inheritance awaits.

For Reflection:

"Blessed are the meek, for they will inherit the earth."

How has "me-ness" hindered you from showing meekness to your neighbors?

Our daily prayer: "Lord, help me to go second."

Neighbors and situations to pray for this week:

____

____

____

____

____

____

For Discussion:

1. List several misconceptions regarding those who are meek. How does this contrast with the biblical view of meekness?
2. Name a historical or contemporary example where someone's meek disposition allowed them to gain the trust and influence of their secular peers.
3. Share any personal experience you've had with the prosperity gospel or New Age teaching. How have these views shaped you in big or small ways?
4. Which example of Jesus' meekness do you find most surprising? What positive impact would it make if you embraced this posture toward your neighbors? Are there any negative impacts you fear?
5. How does knowing that the meek inherit the earth change our demeanor, stewardship of time, and decision-making? How does this future inheritance shape our attitude toward our neighbors now?

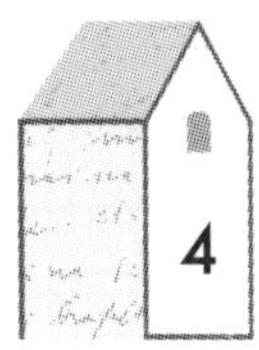

Not Just a Drive-thru

Jesus said: "Blessed are those who hunger and thirst for righteousness, for they will be filled."

The world says: "Blessed are the autonomous, for they will be filled up from all their me-time."

We try not to covet the tall, towering trees in older, established neighborhoods but it's not easy. Way back when we first moved into our neighborhood, we were one of the first of several hundred houses, so every lot started treeless. We had three spindly-looking sticks that were planted around our yard, but it wasn't enough. Chris called me a pacing lioness anytime I would march back-and-forth in our little living room, scheming over how to get a tree line. I began researching trees and their benefits, finding my favorites, and proudly referring to myself as a dendrologist. I was determined that one day, our neighborhood would be filled with beautiful trees. So, it was no surprise to Chris when, five years in, I decided to throw an Arbor Day party. Though Chris initially told me I'd have more luck getting neighbors to an encyclopedia party, in the end, it was glorious and remains one of our favorite gatherings.

We partnered with the Department of Conservation and ordered saplings by the bundle so neighbors could mix and match ten trees for six dollars—Sycamores, White Pines, Silver Maples, Norway Spruces, Dogwoods, and Redbuds. We had fruit and bran muffins and dirt pudding with gummy worms. One neighbor organized a sensory table where kids could see inside a birdhouse gourd, smell and taste various herbs, count tree rings, and play with worms before planting the seed of their choice (pumpkin, carrot, lettuce, or watermelon) in some potting soil. Another neighbor set up a "share-the-wealth" table for those who wanted to exchange bulbs, plants, or veggies. One Chinese family brought some Eastern melon seeds to share. We concluded the event with a five-minute "tree education time" and a tree planting ceremony. Three hundred and forty-five saplings were planted from that gathering and I recall sassily looking at Chris afterward and chanting the words, "Ain't no party like an Arbor Day party cuz an Arbor Day party don't stop."

Watching our redbuds and relationships grow in the seven years since then has been so, *so* satisfying.

Rolling Up our Sleeves

They say when you hit forty, your metabolism isn't what it used to be, though I (Chris) am not sure I ever really liked mine. Recently, I got roped into doing a "Dad Bod" challenge with a bunch of other guys from our church which has resulted in some intermittent fasting. I've learned all sorts of things, including that I don't like to feel hungry. I loathe it, actually. Forgetting the many health benefits, I wonder why I'd choose to be hangry when I could instead choose a bagel with cream cheese or spaghetti or pistachio ice cream ... I'm a tortured soul.

Hunger was a common problem in Jesus' day. When he said, "Blessed are those who hunger and thirst for righteousness, for they will be filled," there were likely those present who were fatigued from a degree of food insecurity. The poor and marginalized were flocking to Jesus while struggling to make ends meet under the heavy burden of Roman taxation. It's likely there were hungry and thirsty listeners that day who weren't fasting by choice. They understood the meaning of hunger in ways most of us never have and would have given just about anything for a good, satisfying meal. All this flavored the way they heard this mouth-watering beatitude and for many, the hunger and thirst metaphor hit hard.

In this fourth beatitude, Jesus invites us to yearn for rightness around us and be gratified by his good ways. He's addressing our appetites. Jesus wants us to experience the *craving for* and *satisfaction from* doing his good will in the same way someone who hasn't eaten for a few days knows the delight of a good meal. There's a refinement of our palates where we relish his law of love and can no longer stomach the spoilage in our neighborhoods. This appetite-switch presents as an eagerness, readiness, and willingness to demonstrate God's character to our neighbors so they can see what he's like. We feel stirred and antsy to honor God. We can't get enough; we're ready to roll up our sleeves and dig into his good works. We're not trying to bite off more than we can chew but we sure want a healthy portion.

Of course, when Jesus said, "Blessed are those who hunger and thirst for righteousness" he wasn't bidding us to crave for acceptance before God.[1] By faith, we have that; it's ours. Left to ourselves, all our "righteous acts are like filthy rags" (Is. 64:6), and no amount of striving to help others is going to change that. But "God made him who had no sin to be sin for us, so that in him we might become the righteousness of God" (2 Cor. 5:21). When Jesus took our sin and traded us his righteousness, he credited us with all of his merits and a whole new identity, with new desires, new motivations, and a new power source. "Therefore, if anyone is in Christ, the new creation has come: The old has gone, the new is here!" (2 Cor 5:17).

We want the righteousness of Christ inside us to change more than our position with God, we want it to change everything. We want it to change our cravings, our desires, and our habits. Jesus' call here is the practical outworking of his righteousness in us—to hunger and thirst for things to be made right around us. It's about us wanting the same things he wants and then getting on and doing them. Our good standing manifests in good works, our tastes begin to change, and there's a hankering for new fruit, the spiritual kind.

So, while Paul says our good works can never save us, he's also clear that we've been created in Christ to do them and he's even prepared them in advance for us (Eph. 2:10). That's what Matthew 5:6 is about. We're made to live out the righteousness of Christ with our neighbors; it's all right there for us. The table is all set, ready to be enjoyed.

Soul Starved

The author of Chronicles gives us examples of both good-doers and wrong-doers, including among Israel's kings. King Hezekiah is a great example of someone who hungered to do right and flourished in the process:

> In everything that he undertook in the service of God's temple and in obedience to the law and the commands, he sought his God and worked wholeheartedly. And so he prospered (2 Chron. 31:21).

Judah's previous king had left God's people vulnerable to external threats and in a state of moral disrepair, so Hezekiah's virtuous leadership was timely. He brought spiritual reform, restoring the temple, removing the places of idolatry, and reinstating the celebration of Passover. He also brought social reform, creating a food distribution system, opening the storehouses, and calling for freewill offerings to provide for those in need of food (2 Chron. 31). If that wasn't enough, he redirected a fresh-water spring into a tunnel he built to ensure his people had water, particularly in times of attack. The more he got, the more he gave.

As Hezekiah hungered and thirsted to do what was good and right, to righteously meet the spiritual and physical needs of those around him, he prospered. Think for a minute how it might have felt for this twenty-five-year-old, who'd taken over a nation in spiritual and social shambles, to walk into these good works that God had created in advance for him. Imagine the satisfaction it brought him to know that he designed a system to provide his people with food and water and was pointing them to a God who could feed them forever.

Years later, Hezekiah's son took over at the same age, but spoiler alert: things didn't go well this time. It's a sad story that stars Manasseh as one of the most unrighteous kings in Israel's history, informing us that righteous parents don't always have righteous kids. Whereas Hezekiah had sought to put things right, Manasseh followed his heart and did what was right in his own eyes. He came in with a very different vision from his dad's, one that prioritized his own wants and values at the expense of his people. He binged on spiritual junk food and got into some dark magic, making his bed with necromancers, and going so far as to ritually kill two of his own sons. His faith-deficiency affected more than his own family; it affected all the neighborhoods in Judah.

Despite his ultimate repentance, he is remembered as someone too caught up in his own self-agenda to be bothered by the needs of his people. Rather than filling his planner with good deeds, he gratified his desires of the moment. But his "freedom" from God took him captive in more ways than one and he left his people more vulnerable than ever.

It turns out selfishness doesn't satisfy.

The Idol Police

It never crossed our minds to build relationships in our previous, highly transient neighborhood. We had two kids under two, whose nursery shared a wall with the condo adjacent to us. At the most inconvenient times, their place would reverberate with nightclub-like bass vibrations, and we'd be putting babies down to the fast-paced, aggressive beats of their electronic dance music. Another neighbor had an unpleasant-looking poltergeist painted on the side of their car and a website for their paranormal society.

I doubt we would have picked up a neighboring book back then. Subconsciously we probably assumed we'd have little in common with our rave-loving or paranormal neighbors. Since there was no apparent benefit to us, it would've seemed more of an inconvenience than an investment to get to know them.

But reflecting on the way Hezekiah and Manasseh interacted in their communities gives us pause. Given our tendency to self-identify with heroes rather than villains, it's important to honestly evaluate our good intentions and our lousy ones. A grace-based theology enables us to be convicted and challenged by Hezekiah's appetite for righteousness, rather than be impressed by it. A posture that's poor in spirit helps us see that Manasseh was caught up in himself as much as fortune-telling, and we can learn from his mistakes, too.

No one likes to be around the idol police, but a little soul-searching never hurt anyone. We may not practice idolatry on the high places as described in 2 Chronicles, but as Tim Keller says, we all have our own "counterfeit gods."[2] We know our phones, comfort, politics, and families can all be idols. But one false god that maybe doesn't get enough negative press is the idol of individualism, and it's causing us spiritual malnutrition.

This is important to address because when Jesus asserts, "Blessed are those who hunger and thirst for righteousness," this is not merely a call to set things right in our own lives, but also in our surrounding communities. When we yearn to see our neighborhoods flourish as God intends, we get caught up in more than our personal piety; we find ourselves on mission, concerned for the people around us, too. This fourth beatitude offers purpose and satisfaction from a communal kind of caring, one we don't experience when we just look out for us and ours.

Since none of us go around saying we worship the idol of individualism, here's a litmus test to diagnose whether we're really the communitarians we think we are:

> When you look at your calendar and to-do list, is there discretionary time available for unscheduled needs?
> When you come home, do you prefer to be autonomous and anonymous?
> How do you prioritize your freedom and needs? Your family's needs? Your neighbors' needs?
> Do you see your neighbors' lives as integrally interconnected to yours?
> Is the missional component to your faith essential or supplemental to your growth in Christ?

The idol of individualism showed up in the Garden of Eden and there have been plenty of people willing to pass its torch onto new generations. Even the way we talk about what it means to have a "personal relationship with God" is important. It would do us well to be mindful of the communal element to our faith—to encourage Godward connection and conviction without becoming too singular. While it's good to know for ourselves what and who we believe in, overplaying our independence rather than interdependence can cause deficiency.

Our counterfeit god of individualism perpetuates a scarcity mindset in neighboring; we find ourselves de-emphasizing good works and hoarding our time and resources. We're afraid to love and serve our neighbors because we focus on what we lack or might lose.

Blessed are the autonomous, we assume, *for they will be filled up from all their me-time.*

Here, our counterfeit beatitude tells us to keep our faith-lives separate from our home-lives because we have our own cups that need filling with me-time. After all, we can't pour out of an empty cup. *What are we, our neighbor's keeper?!*

Hungering and thirsting for righteousness is one of God's ways of addressing this inner idol of autonomy. Just as financial giving is a way to demonstrate our thankfulness and hope in God's provision, practicing righteousness toward our neighbors is a way to demonstrate that it's not all about us. Giving targets our idol of money; doing his heavenly will in our neighborhoods gets at our idol of self-dom. Both can be hard to do when we have bad appetites and are stuffed with the wrong stuff. Left to our scarcity mindsets, no matter how heavenly minded we are, we'll be of no earthly good.

The idol police can make us aware of our time-hoarding and self-serving tendencies but can't save or change us. Paul tells us that, "through the law we become conscious of our sin" (Rom. 3:20) and that until faith came, "we were held in custody under the law, locked up" (Gal. 3:23). Kind of sounds like Manasseh before God changed his heart.

We think our idol of autonomy will give us freedom but ironically it enslaves us. Jesus came to set us free for real.

Umami Bombs

I (Chris) crave Thai food—specifically Pad Thai, Pad See Ew, Pad Kee Mao. Okay yes, they're all noodle dishes but they have something else in common—the ever-trendy umami taste. Umami is Japanese for "savory" or "delicious," and is commonly referred to as the fifth flavor after bitter, salty, sweet, and sour.[3] It's found in crusty, caramelized bits of meats, soy and fish sauces, aged cheeses, truffles and mushrooms, tomatoes and sweet potatoes, olives, kimchi, miso paste, and salty broths. Also, bacon. Once you discover it, it's easy to geek out over the food science behind "umami bombs," where certain food combinations (such as black garlic risotto) unlock "umami synergy" with "eight times the flavor." Umami-less foods now feel bland to me, and I crave that rich, savory, so-good-it's-hard-to-describe taste. I'm getting hungry just thinking about some bleu cheese over a grilled steak or a tomato soup topped with parmesan cheese ...

When Jesus promises satisfaction for those who hunger and thirst after righteousness, he's talking umami-bomb kind of fulfillment. The eight-times-the-flavor kind. We are guaranteed to enjoy his good kingdom work for eternity ... *and* in part now.

The psalmists agree: "I will be fully satisfied as with the richest of foods; with singing lips my mouth will praise you" (Ps. 63:5); "for he satisfies the thirsty and fills the hungry with good things" (Ps. 107:9).

We've probably thought about many of the ways he delights us—whether with his comforting presence through prayer, the provision of a good night's sleep, or through the rich fellowship of close friends—but we may not have considered the deep satisfaction that comes from indulging in good works in our neighborhoods the way Jesus did when he was here.

Imagine the joy Jesus had in putting things right, whether through big healings or small conversations. Think of the smile on Jesus' face, sitting at Matthew's neighborhood dinner party (Mt. 9:10), knowing their grace-filled interactions would drive this tax collector to pen the first Gospel. He knew the deep-seated joy of shocking lepers when he reached out his hand and touched those who hadn't been touched in years (Mt. 8:3). He delighted in staying up late so he could rock Nicodemus's religious paradigm (Jn. 3:1–21). After inviting himself for dinner, he knew the gift of watching one day's table talk shift Zacchaeus's priorities so that he gave half of his possessions away to the poor (Lk. 19:1–9).

These good works bring more than just nice feelings, though that happens, too. Jesus intentionally engineered our neurotransmitters to release and reward us with happy feelings when we do good. Still, he's pointing us, along with Isaiah, to the day when those feelings won't fade and the reward will last:

> Listen, listen to me, and eat what is good,
>   and you will delight in the richest of fare.
> Give ear and come to me; listen, that you may live.
> I will make an everlasting covenant with you,
>   my faithful love promised to David (Is. 55:2–3).

Jesus knew that every one of his interactions mattered. Each time he righted wrongs, he held little rehearsal dinners with samplings of his food finale, where he teased the "wedding supper of the Lamb" (Rev. 19:9) when "the Lord Almighty will prepare a feast of rich food for all peoples, a banquet of aged wine—the best of meats and the finest of wines" (Is. 25:6).

Every righteous act was a sneak peek toward the day when all will be right at last. His actions demonstrated God's generous and just character. He was busy with good works that previewed the coming curse-reversal in a very forthright way: healing, casting out demons, and overpowering death. Jesus didn't see his time here as a drive-thru and we can learn from his example no matter how long we're in our neighborhoods. If it's six-months, two years or ten, we can be satisfied with tiny rehearsal dinners when we do good in small ways, like engaging with our too-loud neighbors or picking up trash or taking a welcome basket to a new neighbor.

The prophet Jeremiah gave the Israelites a similar charge for their seventy-year stay in Babylon, knowing it'd be an intermittent move:

> This is what the LORD Almighty, the God of Israel, says to all those I carried into exile from Jerusalem to Babylon: "Build houses and settle down; plant gardens and eat what they produce … Also, seek the peace and prosperity of the city to which I have carried you into exile. Pray to the LORD for it, because if it prospers, you too will prosper" (Jer. 29:4–5, 7).

Regardless of how long we stay, we seek and find welfare in our neighborhoods when we see the ought nots—the disconnection and depression, the prejudice and marginalization—and partner with Jesus to undo it. We experience joy when we put our phones and AirPods away for a bit and embrace ordinary acts like taking cookies next door or sharing our extra produce with someone nearby. We benefit when our neighborhoods flourish and every curse-reversing dinner party and Spirit-filled conversation matters. Especially Arbor Day parties.

Salty Seasoning

Smart people have a back-up plan for when they get locked out of their house. Smart people take their keys with them when they walk outside. Smart people hide an extra key somewhere. We aren't smart people.

Our garage door decided it would be a good day to stop opening and, with our keys inside and our in-laws out of town, we had no way of driving ourselves to their house to get the spare we'd given them. The couple who lived a few doors down at the time were fairly private people, but we reluctantly knocked on their door to see if they were home. We hated to be an inconvenience, but we also needed help.

Fortunately, they graciously answered the door and our request to help us get our key. It was on that drive that they shared about the recent loss of a family member. In-between churches at the time, they didn't have a Christian community to lean on for support. I asked for their permission to reach out to our church's hospitality team to provide them with some extra meals during their time of mourning. They couldn't believe it when every other day for more than two weeks, meals were dropped off by people from a church they didn't attend. Eventually, they began sitting a few rows across from us and haven't looked back.

Good works taste good to both us and our neighbors.

Our neighbors want to see that, as Christ-followers, we care and are willing to set wrong things right. It makes an impact when we show we're not okay with them handling their stress alone or when we clean up wind-blown trash and try to reverse treelessness. Our neighbors notice when we collaborate to address safety concerns and fix the fact that we're all suffering from loneliness. When we roll up our sleeves in these kinds of ways, we whet their appetite for God because he cares about those things, too. Jesus says it's these Godward actions that cause our neighbors with empty stomachs to glorify their Father in heaven (Mt. 5:16).

What about our response to the 40 million adults in America who are dechurching today?[4] Does it sit right with us that 16 percent of the American adult population is rapidly removing themselves from houses of worship? In contrast to dechurching "casualties" many are doing so "casually," and one of the biggest reasons why …? They've moved. Research is showing that many fall out of the habit due to some major life event, including a move to a new house where they simply haven't plugged in, yet. They would … but they aren't. If we're troubled by this, it may also encourage us to know they claim they want to be invited back and would come if asked. Putting our fourth beatitude to action, when someone new moves into the neighborhood, amidst providing a welcome basket with some practicalities like disposable plates and utensils, a universal screwdriver set, and local carryout menus, we could provide a list of recommended doctors, dentists, cable providers, and a few churches within a 15-minute drive. It's not right that so many are leaving our churches, and while we can't bring 40 million adults back to church with us, we can do for one what we wish we could do for all.

Our role as salt and light is to help our neighbors "taste and see that the LORD is good" (Ps. 34:8). This happens when we shift our personal relationship status with God and go public. Then as Jesus is changing and satisfying our cravings for good God-things, these counter-values begin to waft across rural and suburban fences, up urban apartment stairwells, making our neighbors hungry for him, too.

You could think of each act of neighborliness as an amuse-bouche, a bite-sized appetizer that's served as a surprise. It doesn't take much to make a tasteful impression. In a world of over-scheduling and indifference toward others, a little goes a long way.

For example, a few years ago, we knew there were some struggling middle and high school students in our neighborhood. So, on a day when school was out, we offered to do a personalized coffee run. Granted, there were some complicated drink orders, but you would've thought we were passing out hundred-dollar bills based on the reaction. One single dad with a vastly different lifestyle and worldview reached out shortly thereafter asking if we could put his son on our "prayer chain."

One spring, during a tornado warning, we offered up our basement as a gathering place for anyone who didn't feel safe. Among those who came was a man from a Taoist background who shared that night about his ongoing battle with cancer. I (Chris) got to pray with him, and afterwards we were able to bring him a meal. He later told me that this was a big shift from years of Christianity leaving a bad taste in his mouth.

Typically, we gather in early December for our annual Neighborhood Holiday Open House. We do cookies, hot chocolate, and pictures with Santa. When our neighbors, Dane and Diana, began taking in foster kids, they asked if they could incorporate a service element as well. Diana was able to organize twenty-five families ahead of time to participate in a program called The Giving Tree, and rather than attend the party empty-handed, neighbors brought bikes, instruments, shoes, toys, and clothes according to local children's wish lists. Since this initial effort, we've brainstormed other ways to partner with our local foster and adoption program, doing pajama and dollar drives in conjunction with other gatherings and donating beds, car seats, and strollers to local foster parents. Diana wasn't in the neighborhood for long, but others have led in her absence, and over seven years later, her legacy of righteousness continues.

These weren't radical gestures on our part. It simply struck us that it wasn't right that our next-door teenagers felt alone, that neighbors felt vulnerable when severe weather was imminent, and that local children didn't have toys and clean clothes to wear. But over time, we've seen seemingly insignificant things like coffee runs, tornado shelters, and dollar drives flavor our interactions with the disenchanted and make them curious for Jesus. We'll never forget when we offered a book discussion on *The Purpose Driven Life* and had nearly fifty neighbors sign up.

Something about the combination of good news and good deeds is totally umami.

Let's not grow weary in doing good or lose our saltiness or put our lights under a bowl. Let's let our light shine before our neighbors, so that they may see our good deeds and glorify our Father in heaven. And let's pray expectantly that they'll get a taste of something eternal and join us in coming to Jesus the Bread of Life.

For Reflection:

"Blessed are those who hunger and thirst for righteousness, for they will be filled."

What is a simple, doable step you could take to make something right in your neighborhood this week?

Our daily prayer: "Lord, satisfy me with the good works you have for me in my neighborhood."

Neighbors and situations to pray for this week:

For Discussion:

1. Describe a time when you were really hungry. What food(s) did you crave?
2. How do you interpret Jesus' invitation to hunger and thirst for righteousness? How does this specific language inform your understanding of what it means to show up as a neighbor in your community?
3. In what ways has the promise of individualism left us feeling starved and unsatisfied?
4. What could have been some potential consequences if Jesus had approached his time on earth as merely a "drive-thru" experience rather than engaging in acts of righteousness?
5. How would you define "umami-bomb kind of fulfillment"? How does this enhance your understanding of Jesus' promise to satisfy those who hunger and thirst for righteousness?
6. What actions or initiatives could you see yourself taking that God might use to satisfy you personally while creating curiosity for him among your neighbors?

Forecasting Compassion

Jesus said: "Blessed are the merciful, for they will be shown mercy."

The world says: "Blessed are those who keep score, for they will get what they deserve."

We should say up front that we're animal lovers. Yes, we're the couple who talk in high-pitched voices to our dog Kidani (alternately called Poofy, Boofy, Kapoofy, or Buppy), and let her sleep in our bed with us. But since living in a neighborhood, we've noticed that pets are a controversial topic.

Starting with noise: excessive barking, howling, meowing—these can cause friction amongst neighbors real fast. Damage to property, like scratching a neighbor's fence or digging up a yard is another tension-driver. Aggressive behavior like attacking or biting is a serious problem but even growling can cause some neighbors fear and distress. For neighbors who don't share the same fondness of animals as others, friendly pets that jump, seek to greet, or engage in chasing can be perceived as intrusive and disruptive. For neighbors who live in close proximity, animal odors can be off-putting. For those with allergies, pets are torturesome. We've witnessed contentious conversations about unleashed dogs that escape or roam, followed by threats of trapping and calls to animal control centers. We've seen neighbors get heated over the issue of too many pets, exotic pets, or rural animals, like chickens or livestock. And of course, one of the most common ways to ruffle neighbors' feathers: improper or non-disposal of pet waste. That's ten different ways neighbors can get sideways on the issue of pets alone and no doubt there are more.

These pet-related grievances require mercy as do a thousand other interactions.

Taking a U-turn

Our neighbors are well aware that our family has a lot of needs, some of which have evolved over time, and some have stayed the same. There have been times we've needed practical things like diapers, wipes, clothes, meals, babysitting, dog-sitting, plant-watering, butter, eggs, power tools, and someone to get our mail. Our neighbors have been a means of God's mercy to us in these ways, and so many more. We've needed assistance hanging Christmas lights and spreading mulch in our front yard. We've needed the friendship and emotional support of our neighbors during stressful seasons of parenting and with ministry. We've needed them to bear our burdens and help us process personal difficulties we've faced. We've needed mercy for our self-preoccupation, planting trees close to their property lines, all the cars parked outside on Sunday nights for our church small group, and for the hundreds of shoes our kids have left in their yards and driveway.

We know how much our neighbors need mercy because we need it so badly ourselves.

Our need for compassion comes in various shapes and forms—physical, emotional, spiritual, and more.[1] Sometimes it's visible, sometimes not. Two streets over, an empty nester is coping with osteoporosis. Our widowed neighbor on the corner misses her husband, and the family down the street needs mercy as they manage a house full of teenagers. We know some neighbors are navigating things like narcolepsy, social phobias, and identity issues; others are homebound. Mercy is needed in every household.

But is mercy much different from Jesus' previous invitations, or do they all just bleed together?

This is where we realize that delving into the beatitudes is comparable to examining different facets of a diamond. The more you look, the more you see resemblance and correlation, while also appreciating the particular slant each gives on Jesus' countercultural values. Together the beatitudes serve as refractions for reinterpreting reality in our neighborhoods.

So, as Jesus tilts his beatitude diamond toward the mercy-facing side, we're not surprised to see congruent themes with the previous facets. We've already been thinking about our needs, wants, emotions, and affections, and Jesus has challenged our faith both as a posture and practice.

With mercy, he shows us another angle of the diamond. Right at the intersection of meekness and righteousness, mercy shows us how to feel. And whereas being poor in spirit requires admitting needs, mercy involves meeting them.

So here is our fifth contradiction: flourishing for the merciful. This one is truly disruptive to our sense of fairness and love for accountability. But Jesus wants to redefine and broaden our view of justice, opening possibilities for restoration and reconciliation, prioritizing relationships over rights.

Mercy moves us; it is touched by needs, gaps, and vulnerabilities. It's softened by lack, limits, bruises, and bumps. The merciful are willing to be stirred, swayed, and tugged. There is blessing and flourishing for those with changed hearts and changed minds.

Mercy is the U-turn beatitude. It chooses empathy over what's expected, understanding over indifference, and tenderness rather than repercussion. It withholds judgment and draws near instead. It's willing to modify its plans in attempts to repair and rebuild because it believes in fresh starts and new beginnings.

Mercy sees potential.

Unlike the old saying, "just deserts," referring to dry land with little rainfall as "the punishment that one deserves,"[2] mercy comes in contrast with its non-transactional nature. It is granted freely and does not seek recompense. Despite what is warranted, the slate is wiped clean. It is compassion without compensation.

Jesus illustrated this when he told the parable of the Good Samaritan. A Jerusalem local was attacked, stripped, beaten, and left for dead while en-route to Jericho. Two passing religious leaders crossed over to the other side of the cul-de-sac, before a compassion-filled Samaritan arrived on the scene. He provided immediate first aid—applying oil, wine, and bandages to the man's wounds. After transporting him to a place of temporary housing where he could rest and heal, he paid the innkeeper for his stay and opened a line of credit, promising to pay any extra expenses or debt on the Jewish man's behalf (Lk. 10:30–35).

When Jesus asked which of the three bystanders was a neighbor to the man in need, "The expert in the law replied, 'The one who had mercy on him.' Jesus told him, 'Go and do likewise'" (Lk. 10:37).

Imagine how disorienting it would have been for this man to awaken in a strange bed in a strange motel. Imagine his earnestness to learn the identity of the one who'd saved his life. And then imagine the look on his face as the innkeeper explained that the mystery mercy-man was someone with whom he shared a deep-seated religious and racial conflict. His rival had chosen to become his neighbor.

Jesus offers a mercy that meets needs but also makes amends. It unsticks us where we're stuck and upsets our rhythms of reciprocity in the very best way. It overthrows our passion for merit, our tendency toward retribution, and is refreshing to both the giver and receiver.

This upside-down kindness is meant to be passed on. God interrupts our lives with compassion, therefore we can show compassion. God forgives our debts, therefore we can forgive others. The apostle Paul beats this drum again and again:

> If you're a hard worker and do a good job, you deserve your pay; we don't call your wages a gift. But if you see that the job is too big for you, that it's something only *God* can do, and you trust him to do it—you could never do it for yourself no matter how hard and long you worked—well, that trusting-him-to-do-it is what gets you set right with God, *by* God. Sheer gift (Rom. 4:4–5, MSG).

> Bear with each other and forgive one another if any of you has a grievance against someone. Forgive as the Lord forgave you (Col. 3:13).

The Revenge Button

Our counselor didn't hold out any promise for repair as we began processing some longtime relational hurts, but when I (Elizabeth) saw the cover of the book she had assigned for homework, I was pleasantly surprised. The blurb referred to having boundaries with difficult people. However, about 100 pages in, I turned to Chris in horror, my book all tear-stained, saying: "She tricked us! This isn't the book I wanted—this is a book on forgiveness!"

Mercy wasn't in the forecast, yet it broke through and transformed us all.

The term emotional forecasting, or affective forecasting, refers to the process of predicting your emotional reaction to specific experiences or circumstances. It estimates future feelings based on current beliefs and expectations. This concept was developed and popularized by two American Psychologists, Wilson and Gilbert, while researching for the National Institute of Mental Health. They measured the accuracy with which we can anticipate our emotions, whether the emotion will be negative or positive, and its intensity and duration. After much research, they determined that we are just not very good at predicting our emotional reactions to circumstances.[3]

They later joined social psychologist, Kevin Carlsmith, to examine how emotional forecasting correlates to one experience in particular: revenge.[4] Previous studies had shown that the pleasure portion of one's brain lit up when participants were able to take revenge toward someone who had wronged them in a game. But these measurements had been taken one minute prior to the punishment-making decision, so it was inconclusive whether punishment was truly pleasurable.[5]

So, the question remained: Is revenge really rewarding? Or had these predictions gone wrong? Their findings were fascinating.

They ran three revenge scenarios in which subjects could choose to punish other participants for what they deemed bad behavior … or not. These were interactive games where players could earn money if they cooperated. Unbeknownst to them, there were staged "free riders," who could earn more and make others earn less, causing everyone frustration. However, despite predicting that some punitive action would repair their moods, those who chose retaliation against the free riders found retribution had the opposite effect. The punishers felt angry immediately afterward and were still ruminating ten minutes later.[6] Any short-term satisfaction from revenge was gone in a minute, and they were left feeling worse than before, whereas those who chose not to punish the free riders moved on much more quickly.

Jesus was onto something; our bodies are proof.

Furthermore, in their discussion about why the punishers felt so bad, the researchers had several theories, but this one stood out: "the negative impact of punishment may stem from the fact that participants had, so to speak, to thrust the knife themselves, which may have violated their sense that they were good people who do not harm others."[7]

The punishers wanted to punish without being the punishing-type.

Maybe that's why karma has such wide appeal. We want people to get what we think they deserve but we don't want to have to push the button. Wanting karma for our neighbors is kind of like hoping for a cosmic hitman—our role is removed but our hearts are retaliatory. If they've wronged us in some way, we can stand back as spectators, maintaining our sense of self-righteousness while rooting for them to face the boomerang of their consequences. They get the hammer while we remain honorable.

The Jews listening that day on the mountainside had been steeped in a tit for tat, merit-based culture. Jesus was shattering that paradigm:

> You have heard that it was said, "Eye for eye, and tooth for tooth." But I tell you, do not resist an evil person. If anyone slaps you on the right cheek, turn to them the other cheek also. And if anyone wants to sue you and take your shirt, hand over your coat as well. If anyone forces you to go one mile, go with them two miles. Give to the one who asks you, and do not turn away from the one who wants to borrow from you (Mt. 5:38–42).

Jesus is *not* saying we should minimize assaults or tolerate ongoing abuse. Rather this is his answer to our moralistic bent. He knew that inviting us to turn our cheeks, hand over our best coat, and walk two extra miles would overturn our performance-based approach to neighboring. When we think of our neighbors as free riders, just like those early listeners viewed the Romans living among them, we want assurance that justice will prevail—that is justice for everyone but ourselves. Jesus gives us the justice we crave, but not in our way and not on our timetable. He subverts our merit-based mindsets by de-emphasizing entitlement and presenting a radical generosity to the troubled, struggling, and underserved.

The Pharisees thought this was ridiculous. They were more into fairness, as they saw fairness. And since their spiritual résumés were stacked, they could look next door and pat themselves on the back:

> The Pharisee stood by himself and prayed: "God, I thank you that I am not like other people—robbers, evildoers, adulterers—or even like this tax collector. I fast twice a week and give a tenth of all I get" (Lk. 18:11–12).

God's mercy wants to melt this kind of moral superiority. Like this guy, we have poor spiritual E.Q.'s and our prayers need course-correcting. Moralism comes as another counterfeit beatitude and makes us out of touch because we're so busy bolstering, blame-shifting, defending, and deflecting, we become oblivious and desensitized to the needs around us. Jesus calls for a pulse. He makes it clear that he doesn't want negligent neighbors; he wants us to take mercy seriously:

> Woe to you, teachers of the law and Pharisees, you hypocrites! You give a tenth of your spices—mint, dill and cumin. But you have neglected the more important matters of the law—justice, mercy and faithfulness. You should have practiced the latter, without neglecting the former (Mt. 23:23).

Rule-obsessors become painstakingly focused on parsing things out—down to the very last mint leaf—yet they miss the forest for the trees. A quid pro quo system doesn't have room for weightier matters, like mercy. Only those who've struggled themselves, who've felt burdened and unworthy—who've awoken to bandaged wounds and a line of credit—would stand at a distance alongside the tax collector, unable to lift their eyes, beating their chest, saying, "God, have mercy on me, a sinner" (Lk. 18:13).

This kind of posture is hard to fake because our lives are always reminding us what we really believe.

Mercy breaks the cycle.

The Interruptible God

Generally, we see interruptions as inconveniences. They break our focus, disrupt our workflow, and hinder our ability to focus on the task at hand. Car alarms interrupt our quiet, rain interrupts our plans, and text notifications interrupt our conversations. These interferences can be irritating, annoying, and overwhelming.

Not for Jesus. His afternoons were continually being disrupted by questions, kids, friends, and challenges. Here was a repeat notification that would sound all around him: *"Lord have mercy."*

When Bartimaeus, a blind, roadside beggar, heard that Jesus had come to town, he began to shout, "Jesus, Son of David, have mercy on me!" (Mk. 10:47). The more people tried to shut him up, the louder he got. "HAVE MERCY ON ME!!" As a precursor to his healing, we find two extraordinary words: "Jesus stopped" (Mk. 10:49).

Two other blind men followed him in Capernaum with the very same mantra: "Have mercy on us, Son of David!" (Mt. 9:27). When Jesus pulled away for some R&R, he heard it again from a Canaanite woman whose daughter was suffering from a demon:

"Lord, Son of David, have mercy on me!" (Mt. 15:22). The disciples were ready to send her away, but Jesus wasn't. And then there was the father who came on his knees, explaining his son's spiritual seizures: "Lord, have mercy on my son" (Mt. 17:15).

We project our own intolerance of others' needs onto God, but Jesus reveals a mercy that embraces interruptions. Like the Pharisee and the Levite, we don't want to be detoured by someone else's needs or misfortune. Our status reads: "Do Not Disturb."

Although so often not said aloud, there are deep heart calls from those all around us: *"Please, have mercy."* We're unmoved. Our neighbors' needs feel like tangents in our lives, like side notes; we just can't handle anything extra. As our brains make flash decisions about what and who is worthy of our time, neighbors—let alone neighbors with burdens—don't qualify. After all, if we give an inch, they'd take a mile. Who's got time for free riders?

How would it change us to know the God who is not inconvenienced by our needs? Far from feeling sidetracked, Jesus saw needy neighbors as his main mission. He found delight in pausing to extend mercy.

What we consider disruptions, Jesus calls divine appointments.

The Mercy Cycle

The story behind us ending up in our neighborhood is a bittersweet one: our best friends convinced us to move next door. At first it was the things dreams are made of—we went for walks, shared food, watched TV together late at night, and folded laundry together in each other's driveways. But over time, our perfect next-door wishdream[8] began to sour and at the time

I (Elizabeth) couldn't pinpoint why. There was the initial drift, then end-of-life signs, and eventually it was gone. We didn't speak for over three-and-a-half painful years. I cried so many tears during those years—tears of confusion, of devastation, and of heartbreak. Now looking back, I have a much clearer understanding of the factors that led to our friendship funeral, things like my big insecurities and unrealistic expectations, for starters. God was doing a deep work in both our hearts and almost four years later, he miraculously gave us back the friendship—not the same one, but a new one. She forgave me, I forgave her, and with much weeping, God did the unthinkable: we were fully restored.[9]

Mercy was costly for us both, in the giving and in the receiving. In the giving, it required sacrifice of time and energy on both our parts to have those initial difficult conversations because they were taxing. It meant us both relinquishing our perceived rights and letting go of our resentment and the overall sting. It cost us emotional vulnerability to step back into each other's lives, and that was scary. Mercy meant risk and uncertainty. It challenged our deeply ingrained patterns and bid us both to change.

But there was no greater price than the receiving of the mercy from each other because that cost us ... *nothing*. I think we would have both preferred penance because mercy was too humbling.

But at the cost of our pride, here comes the reward. Mercy is the only beatitude where the promise is the same as the blessing. The merciful will receive exactly what they give ... mercy. This is a whole different kind of cycle, and it works like this: God shows us mercy, we receive it, we extend it, we receive it, again.[10] It starts at the cross:

> He forgave us all our sins, having canceled the charge of our legal indebtedness, which stood against us and condemned us; he has taken it away, nailing it to the cross (Col. 2:13–14).

> Once you were not a people, but now you are the people of God; once you had not received mercy, but now you have received mercy (1 Pet. 2:10).

The cross is where God's justice and mercy converge, leveling out every neighbor, every Pharisee and tax collector. Our cries for due process are answered. Jesus bore the wrath of God, including his wrath toward our mercilessness. Despite all our double standards and disinterest toward our neighbors, he bought us back with his blood and made forgiveness possible. We deserve silent withdrawal and worse, but we get a Father who runs to us with mercy.

This is where everything changes. When we're swept into this new cycle, mercy defangs us. It disarms and undermines our self-righteous inclinations. Our inner Pharisee loses its power and appeal. We surrender to a new kind of safety where there's less fear and more compassion. Then it becomes habitual.

Peter wanted to know when it would stop: "Lord, how many times shall I forgive my brother or sister who sins against me? Up to seven times? Jesus answered, "I tell you, not seven times, but seventy-seven times" (Mt. 18:21–22). God's compassion never ends.

In this kind of loop, mercy compounds. The more we experience it, the more we extend it. Jesus explained this to Simon the Pharisee in Luke 7, when he highlighted the love of "the sinful woman" through a short story of canceled debts:

> "Now which of them will love him more?" Simon replied, "I suppose the one who had the bigger debt forgiven." "You have judged correctly," Jesus said (Lk. 7:42–43).

Big experiences of mercy equal big expressions of it.

We want to be caught up in this kind of mercy-circuit so that when it comes time to meet needs and forgive grievances, rather than portion out teaspoons of mercy, we fill buckets with it.

> Be merciful, just as your Father is merciful. Do not judge, and you will not be judged. Do not condemn, and you will not be condemned. Forgive, and you will be forgiven. Give, and it will be given to you. A good measure, pressed down, shaken together and running over, will be poured into your lap. *For with the measure you use, it will be measured to you* (Lk. 6:36–38, emphasis added).

Mercy begets mercy.

A Re-forecast

We are terrible forecasters. We have good reasons for predicting that this kind of neighborhood mercy-ministry will exhaust and deplete us. *Giving, forgiving, giving, forgiving.* We presume neighboring will be a one-way street and fear our neighbors' needs will drain us beyond what we can provide. We worry that our own boundaries will be encroached upon, and we won't be able to say "no" when we need to. Alternatively, an exaggerated sense of responsibility for our neighbors' well-being can backfire—when we think we're the sole person responsible for our neighbors' welfare, we want out.

It's true that mercy asks a lot of us—it requires sacrifice and generosity when we don't feel like it. It opens us up when we want to close off, and that's not always fun. But we underestimate its reciprocal nature; our neighbors are God's means of mercy in our lives, too.

I (Chris) think about specific neighbors whose kids are being bullied at school, others who are travel-weary from frequent time away, some contemplating divorce, others who can't get along. These very neighbors who've needed mercy themselves, have also been the very ones to extend it to us when we've needed it just as much.

Imagine a re-forecast. How might it change our projections if our data was more mercy-based? If we stepped out of our moralistic narratives and updated our info? How would it change our guess-timations … and us?

Would we still grimace at the thought of serving, or would we be quicker to lend our struggling neighbors a helping hand? Would we continue to resist compassion when wronged, or would we bury the hatchet once and for all?

Jesus is inviting us to anticipate what mercy will do, to consider the healing and joy we'll find when we show up at home. He wants us to re-estimate all the future outcomes in our neighborhood through this lens of flourishing. We would never have seen mercy coming but Jesus gives us a new outlook.

Blessed are the merciful, for they will receive mercy.

For Reflection:

"Blessed are the merciful, for they will receive mercy."

What needs do your neighbors have that you could meet right now? What amends do you need to make?

Our daily prayer: "Lord, sweep me into your mercy cycle."

Neighbors and situations to pray for this week:

For Discussion:

1. Share about a time when you received mercy. What impact did it have on you?
2. Summarize how biblical mercy "meets needs but also makes amends." How does this twofold understanding of mercy act as a transformative U-turn in the lives of both the giver and the receiver?
3. In the psychology experiment researching revenge, what were the outcomes for those who chose to retaliate against the "free riders"? What were their motivations or expectations? How did the actual outcomes differ from their initial hopes?
4. What insights do we gain about the nature of Jesus' mercy by considering his willingness to be interrupted?
5. Explain the mercy cycle. In what ways can we cultivate patterns of mercy that break the cycles of transactional relationships and promote deeper connections with our neighbors?
6. Name one current need for mercy in your own life. What is a practical need for mercy you could meet in a neighbor's life (either in giving or forgiving)?

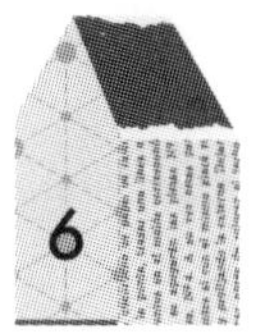

Be Whole and Behold

Jesus said: "Blessed are the pure in heart, for they will see God."

The world says: "Blessed are those who maintain public and private persona, for no one will see what's really going on inside."

We could tell you we have a home orchard, and we wouldn't technically be lying. Perhaps you would naively envision a picturesque little property with cheery rows of flowering canopies or delightful lines of trees packed with apples or plums, calling you to take a stroll and fill a basket to your heart's content. Our home orchard isn't exactly like that. Okay, it's not an orchard at all. But we do have a small hill that stretches down the side of our house that holds five humble fruit trees: two pear, two apple, and one self-pollinating peach tree.

Over the course of the few years we've had them, we've harvested a few peaches and some small, misshaped apples and pears. On the surface, not too impressive. But to us, a thrilling bounty. We love those trees.

But then there's the *other* pear tree, the self-important, shifty Aristocrat pear who tricked us with its noble name and promised to be the ornamental star of our backyard. The tree farmers assured us this cousin to the Bradford pear was fast-growing and would develop into a tall, strong, flowering beauty. After a quick Google image search of Aristocrat pears on our phones, we were sold.

It wasn't until years later that a neighbor gently made us aware of the curse on pear trees that don't bear pears. Although very popular, these seemingly innocent trees are invasive nightmares. The fluffy strips of white blossoms you might see in suburban parts of the country are variants of Callery pear trees, and in the last fifteen years or so they have blasted onto the scene along edges of roadways by cross pollinating and greedily choking out native species. Worse, they are disease-resistant and form impenetrable thickets with four-inch-long thorns, making them a hazard to animals and almost impossible to remove.

We'd been duped.

We were Googling an alias but had we searched Callery trees, we would have seen the thorns. We would have read headlines such as "The Rise and Fall of the Callery Tree" and "The Curse of the Bradford Pear" and "Callery Pears: Not Recommended." We would have seen that many conservation departments offer rewards to anyone willing to remove these monsters from their yards. We had no idea our beloved tree was a villain who we would eventually name Prince Hans of the Southern Isles for his doubleness.

Our tree was a hypocrite. It claimed to be a pear tree, but it didn't bear pears. It was a phony, a pretender—a pear tree in name only. Not only that, but it also did great damage to all in its way. Its beauty was skin-deep—charming and flashy on the outside, but inside an infectious troublemaker.

Kind of sounds like what we read toward the end of the Sermon on the Mount:

> By their fruit you will recognize them. Do people pick grapes from thornbushes, or figs from thistles? Likewise, every good tree bears good fruit, but a bad tree bears bad fruit. A good tree cannot bear bad fruit, and a bad tree *cannot* bear good fruit. Every tree that does not bear good fruit is cut down and thrown into the fire. Thus, by their fruit you will recognize them (Mt. 7:16–20, emphasis added).

Jesus would never have bought that tree.

What You See

Perhaps our duplicitous little tree, or "Hans" if you will, has something to teach us about what it means to be neighbors who are pure in heart. You see, non-fruit-bearing pear trees identify in name with something good while producing something bad.[1] Not only do they mislead us, these beauties betray us by spreading ruin and disorder through their nearly invisible seed. We don't know it's happening until it's too late.

Jesus had this habit of peeling back the bark of our hearts and revealing what's below the surface. He isn't interested in skin-deep disciples or actors who can go through the motions without engaging their real selves. He wants lovers and followers, not company people.

He wants our whole hearts, and he wants them to be whole.

That's what being pure in heart is all about. It's Jesus' call to "holiness as wholeness,"[2] his invitation to grow into fully integrated people, where our insides match our outsides.[3] It's his appeal for raw honesty and clean consciences, because there's no need for hiding. Purity of heart means there's consistency between our inner life and our outer life. Our invisible thoughts, feelings, values, and motivations are in congruence with our words and outward actions.

Kenneth Bailey describes purity of heart this way: "What you see is what you get … [believers] have one motive for what they do, and they harbor no hidden agenda."[4] When our hearts are pure, they're not fragmented; they're all in one piece. We're trusting God to bring all parts of our lives together, so we can be one undivided, unfractured person. This beatitude is a call to a whole-person devotion where we give Christ access to transform our darkest thoughts and our biggest feelings.

We're not Christians in name only; we are called to an ever-increasing, singular love for Christ that shows up. Pear trees bear pears. Christian neighbors bear love, joy, peace, patience, kindness, goodness, faithfulness, gentleness, and self-control.

And those around us are looking for this purity of heart. A number of years ago, we were hanging out with some neighbors. We didn't know each other very well at the time, and so it was a surprise when, out of the blue the husband turned to me (Elizabeth) and asked, "What is your church like exactly?" We asked some follow-up questions and found that he wasn't looking for information on service times and kids' groups that day; he wanted a vibe. Is this a "make-a-difference-in-your-life" kind of church or the lip service type? Does your faith in Jesus impact your marriage and parenting? Is it real? Is it pure in heart, or is it compartmentalized?

A Discreet Counterpart

To really understand purity of heart, we need to understand its dark counterpart, hypocrisy. Headlines are full of all kinds of examples of Christian leaders who haven't practiced what they've preached. It happens so often that we're almost desensitized to it. Deleted text messages, hidden travel receipts, blackmail, extortion, affairs … There's secrecy and lying to cover the gap between what one has said and done. We believed the lie: Blessed are those who have public and private persona, for no one will see what's really going on inside.

You might think this is the only sort of doubleness that shadows as our counterfeit beatitude. But there's a specific brand of hypocrisy Jesus highlights here in the book of Matthew that's more discreet.[5] It's not just found in megachurch documentaries about high-profile pastors and covered scandals. If that was it, all us non-celebrity Christians who aren't cheating or stealing would get a pass. But no, the hypocrisy emphasized here is much less memorable and we typically take it far less seriously. It's the duality between the authentic version of ourselves and our copy, the disconnect between what we really think, feel, want, love, and hate—and what we present.

Recently, we came back from vacation and were both feeling scattered and unfocused as we adjusted back to normal life. Why the haze? Some post-holiday blues are normal, but this felt especially disorienting. We found ourselves compulsively talking about the "next time" we could get away again as a family, not wanting to admit our anxious feelings might be a symptom of a desire to escape normal life. When we followed the feelings of antsiness, we found an altar to a counterfeit rest. Vacation was king and we were left disenchanted until we could see him again.

When we are not wholly God's, our hearts are not whole. And when our hearts are not whole, we are not good neighbors. Sure, we might be all cordial on the outside, but if inside we are yearning to be elsewhere, if we are secretly annoyed at our neighbors, or looking down on them in some way, we are not really loving them at all.

Even while writing this section, I (Chris) just received a grouchy text from a neighbor regarding an upcoming neighborhood event. It struck me as curmudgeonly and rubbed me the wrong way. Sure, I sent a cordial text back. My words were gracious enough and I said all the right things to defuse the situation, but if I'm honest, I'm judgey. Outwardly, I'm just fine and smile and nod, but inwardly I'm stewing, labeling, blaming, and making unfair assumptions, all ironically while writing a chapter about being pure in heart.

This is the type of neighborly doubleness Jesus wants to unseat. It's the polarity between our internal and external lives in Christ, the neighbors we are outside our homes and inside them. He wants those two to be the same. Jesus rehashes this later: "These people honor me with their lips, but their hearts are far from me" (Mt. 15:8).

Do our words and actions match the receipts of our private thoughts and feelings?

> When our social media feeds show us a picture of other neighbors all hanging out without us, can we post a thoughtful comment and mean it?
> When a neighbor goes on a rant about their candidate, can we genuinely respond saying, "I can see where you're coming from"?

> When we encourage our neighbor regarding their home improvements, are we celebrating with them, or begrudging them?

We can't always wait until our hearts are in the right place before responding to a grumpy text like the one from my neighbor. There are times when we need to stretch those kindness muscles, do the right thing in the moment, and give our hearts space to catch up later. But Jesus is challenging us—*do they catch up? Are we aiming for our hearts and lives to match?*

How do our fractured hearts fracture others?

Upping the Ante

As an introvert, I (Chris) am easily drained by small talk. Don't get me wrong, I enjoy meaningful conversations and discussions with people that go both ways. But it's hard for me to stay engaged when I feel trapped in a one-sided talk with a Chatty Cathy where my being there feels irrelevant.

We all have these people in our lives. We find ourselves trying to avoid those we know will get going on some long monologue. Outwardly, we act interested and fake-it-till-we-make-it, but inwardly we're irked and anxious. We know we should honor our neighbors by listening, but we also want to run for the hills.

So, is the solution to just bow out and/or say what we're really thinking? No. Jesus wants to expose our painfully low expectations of our own hearts and push us to deal with the discrepancies in the ways we interact with those around us:

> You have heard that it was said to the people long ago, "You shall not murder, and anyone who murders will be subject to

> judgment." But I tell you that anyone who is angry with a brother or sister will be subject to judgment. Again, anyone who says to a brother or sister, 'Raca,' is answerable to the court. And anyone who says, 'You fool!' will be in danger of the fire of hell (Mt. 5:21–22).

Great job not killing your neighbor over there—bravo! But what about all the savage thoughts you've had about the way he looks and talks? How about those eye rolls and visceral groans over his property maintenance or how he lets his dog bark at obscene hours of the night? You haven't committed a felony, but you've done away with him in your heart. So you didn't do the worst-case scenario … what about the best-case scenario? You think bare minimum, but I say you're using the wrong grading system.

You think law, I say love.

Inwardly we get defensive when the standard feels too high: *But no one is this pure! No one's this perfect!*

We're six beatitudes in at this point and Jesus has upped the ante too far. As with the others, we object again, but now at the end of our striving, in knee-deep despair we blurt out: *Who can do this??*

The psalmist asks the same question:

> Who may ascend the mountain of the LORD? Who may stand in his holy place? The one who has clean hands and a pure heart, who does not trust in an idol or swear by a false god (Ps. 24:3–4).

Then comes a welcomed newsflash: the psalmist did not have us in mind as the answer to this question. Jesus alone had clean hands and a pure heart. His perfect purity exposes our disparities but when this happens, he offers wide arms.

When we're convicted by the touchy text we sent, the nice message we didn't mean, or the one we should have sent and didn't ... when we look at ourselves and see double ... when we're ashamed of our disingenuous interactions with the next-door chatterbox ... God reminds us he sent his Son for the impure in heart. Jesus died for hypocrites whose faith is skin-deep, who are just going through the motions. When our neighboring is more driven by networking our communities than nurturing them, he extends mercy. He forgives us for teaching verses about loving our neighbors while judging, envying, and ignoring them. With his own blood, he bought loads of double-minded nobodies and turns us into single-hearted somebodies.

All this from the one who knew no such disparity. Rather than twoness, he shows us his trueness.

He was true with his emotions

Jesus didn't put on a happy face or a front when things were hard. When his soul was overwhelmed with sorrow to the point of death, he told his friends (Mt. 26:38) and when he was angry at the moneychangers, he flipped tables (Mt. 21:12). He didn't sugar coat things to maintain his God image. What was on the inside was consistent with what was on the outside.

He was true with his words

Jesus said what he meant and meant what he said. Whether it was through encouragement (Jn. 14:1), instruction (Mt. 18:18–20), challenge (Mt. 19:16–22), or storytelling (Lk. 15:11–32), his words came from the overflow of his heart (Mt. 12:34).

He was true to his associations

Jesus didn't try to keep up appearances. Despite religious leaders being aghast that the woman with the bad reputation would pour her perfume all over Jesus' feet, continually kissing them, he received her gift gladly (Lk. 7:36–50). When he was accused of being a friend to tax collectors and sinners, he didn't argue (Mt. 11:19). He wasn't worried about losing votes or damaging his standing at the club. He valued each and every neighbor, even if others didn't.

He was true to his values

Even when his priorities were unpopular and his convictions made things inconvenient, he stayed true. He healed a man's hand on the Sabbath knowing religious rulers would lose their minds (Mt. 12:9–14). He did this because he cared about his neighbor rather than being a stickler to man-made interpretations to the rules. This value-congruence caused him to walk through the city of Samaria on his way from Judea to Galilee, even though most of his colleagues would go long distances to avoid it (Jn. 4:4). After having just said "God so loved the *world,*" he put his money where his mouth was by demonstrating that all races and backgrounds qualify as those he came to seek and save.

Whereas we may try to excuse or conceal our inconsistencies, Jesus proved his heart was pure, true, and trustworthy. He wasn't artificial or superficial and had no double standard.

He was true every time.

Behold Jesus

We all have longings for revelation, to step into the unseen realm, to go deeper, see further. Gideon asked for a sign and assurance in his battle against the Midianites (Judg. 6:17–22), Moses asked to see God's glory (Ex. 33:18), and David wanted to gaze upon God's beauty (Ps. 27:4). God has set eternity in our hearts (Ecc. 3:11) and because of that, we long for something more. We're hardwired for connection with a transcendent God. We want his manifest presence in our lives, to be encouraged, strengthened, and transformed in his company. We want to sense that he's near and be reminded that he cares about us specifically.

So, the promise for the pure in heart has wide appeal:

> Blessed are the pure in heart, for they will see God (Mt. 5:8).

But what does it mean to see God?

Since God the Father does not have a body, we cannot and will not see him with our physical eyes, not in this lifetime, not in eternity future. Paul describes him as the king, who is "eternal, immortal, [and] invisible" (1 Tim. 1:17). So how in the world can Jesus offer the promise of perceiving an eternal, invisible, immortal being to finite, physical mortals?

One thing we know: Jesus. He was God's special revelation, "the image of the invisible God" (Col. 1:15). When Philip asked to see the Father, Jesus replied: "Don't you know me, Philip, even after I have been among you such a long time? Anyone who has seen me has seen the Father" (Jn. 14:9). Jesus' promise was that the pure in heart would see *him*.

When we follow God with our whole hearts, our warped views of God will be corrected, and Jesus will come into focus. We will see a visible God who drew near to us and still does, who died for us, who cares for our needs, who's defeated death, who's preparing a future home for us, a God who gives meaning, and whose statutes are good.

Our neighbors have eternity set in their hearts, too. Just like us, they long for a transcendent God to interrupt their lives with a sign that he is listening and that he cares. Imagine the difference it would make in our neighborhoods to behold Jesus, to behold someone pure in heart.

But seeing the disparities of our own hearts has us doubtful we could ever offer our neighbors a glimpse into this kind of consistency.

Friends, we are not destined to be hopeless hypocrites. By God's grace, we "are being transformed into his image with *ever-increasing* glory" (2 Cor. 3:18, emphasis added). By trusting God to fuse our fractured hearts, increasingly now and fully in the future, we show our neighbors a great promise. We don't have to be perfect to share our hope for the day when we're no longer skin-deep disciples, torn by multiple loves. We desperately await the time when we'll look in the mirror and rather than see double, we'll see our true selves. We will finally be who we were meant to be.

> Dear friends, now we are children of God, and what we will be has not yet been made known. But we know that when Christ appears, we shall be like him, for we shall see him as he is (1 Jn. 3:2).

We're not quite there yet.

Kintsugi

Sometimes we can get our kids to obey us in public for a very brief and holy moment. But it doesn't last. When we get home, we collapse. The amount of work it takes for all of us to hold it together when we're out, is ... a lot. It's different at home, though. Our neighbors see the disobedience, the temper tantrums, the messes, the yelling. *And that's just Chris.*

In all seriousness, we can't hide at home, but maybe that's a good thing. I (Elizabeth) think I subconsciously used to think "letting my light shine" to my neighbors meant being a good example and representing Christ well. While that's true to a certain extent—this whole chapter has been on hypocrisy versus congruence—for a long time I didn't know how to let out the real me. The real me gets lonely, insecure, ragey toward my kids, and has bouts of doubt. What about those things?

Recently, our neighbor Elena offered to come over and help me paint. While we did, I shared some of what I was processing from our parenting class at church. I opened up about some bad habits I was seeing in myself that I wanted to see God change. After a while, we set down our paint brushes to get a snack, and when we did, she confided in me regarding a deeply personal struggle. From there, she shared with me why she doesn't believe in God and has been so turned off by Christians over the years. Why would someone like Elena, who I've known for six years to be a very private person, choose to share in such an unguarded way?

Paul gives us insight in 2 Corinthians:

> For God, who said, "Let light shine out of darkness," made his light shine in our hearts to give us the light of the knowledge of God's glory displayed in the face of Christ. But we have this treasure in jars of clay to show that this all-surpassing power is from God and not from us (2 Cor. 4:6–7).

When we feel like we have to hide parts of ourselves, our neighbors will go into hiding, too. Thankfully, the opposite is also true. What would happen in our neighborhoods if we took our place as jars of clay? If we imaged ourselves as cracked pots, whole, and "not destroyed," with the light of Jesus coming through?

Makoto Fujimura shares this vision. He is recognized for his abstract expressionism and is considered one of the leading artists of the "slow art" movement. He patiently and deliberately creates pieces that in some cases have taken over twenty years to complete.[6] Not only is his work created in an unhurried fashion, but it's also designed to be appreciated slowly, too. Alongside his other artforms, he is known for the Japanese art of repair called Kintsugi, a technique which mends broken ceramic teaware by applying lacquer and gold in its fissures. Once repaired, these pieces of pottery are often worth more than before they were broken. Fujimura finds the parallels between us and these ceramics striking. He finds beauty in the brokenness of the pot and teaches that God does, too.[7]

Imagine if you slowly started to appreciate the work of God's fusion in your life how your neighbors might also. What if rather than putting on faultless facades, we pointed to our chips and imperfections as evidence of our need for God and his grace? What if that picture of brokenness and wholeness flipped their whole paradigm of who Jesus is and caused them to be curious about him for the first time, or again? Our neighbors are longing to see faith that's true and genuine, faith that makes a difference in our lives. Rather than writing our neighbors off, could we seek points of common ground and accept the real them, too?

Your neighbor is a cracked pot, just like you are, but they need to know the hope of wholeness we have in Christ. Maybe if we showed that we're works in progress, they'd conclude God can draw close to them in all their imperfections too.

For Reflection:

"Blessed are the pure in heart, for they will see God."

What inconsistencies are there in your heart toward your neighbors?

Our daily prayer: "Lord … give me an undivided heart, that I may fear your name" (Ps. 86:11).

Neighbors and situations to pray for this week:

For Discussion:

1. Where do you see hypocrisy in our world? Name some of its effects.
2. What does it mean to be pure of heart? What are the benefits of living as an undivided, unfractured person?
3. How does honesty about our own contradictions and weaknesses allow us to better accept our neighbors and see them as whole individuals?
4. In what four ways does Jesus show purity of heart? Discuss the one that holds the most significance for you personally. How does it capture Jesus' authenticity? How does it call for a consistent inner and outer life?
5. Eternity has been set in both our hearts and our unbelieving neighbors' hearts. How does an awareness of these shared longings influence your desire to build spiritual bridges that help point your neighbors to Jesus?
6. What does the Japanese art of Kintsugi have to teach us about our brokenness? How might acknowledging our imperfections with our neighbors have a positive effect on their spiritual journey and their view of God?

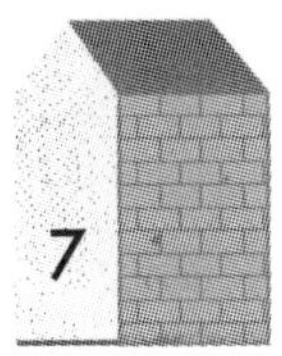

Making a Difference in Difference

Jesus said: "Blessed are the peacemakers, for they will be called children of God."

The world says: "Blessed are those who seek sameness, for they will never have to resolve conflict with anyone."

Before we developed close relationships with our neighbors, I (Elizabeth) felt reasonably secure in my faith convictions, including beliefs about the supernatural, the authority and reliability of Scripture, the exclusivity of Jesus, and other topics that some of my neighbors might have found odd or difficult to accept. However, as we became more integrated into our neighborhood community and developed close relationships with many from differing ideologies, I had this fear of being found out. I was particularly concerned about how some neighbors would react to my views on a couple of issues, including sexual ethics. On more than one occasion, I've had the chance to face my fear and see God preserve peace amidst disagreement.

The first time it happened, I was leading a neighborhood book discussion with a few ladies on a book by Christian psychiatrist Dr. Henry Cloud. In it, he made the distinction between accepting someone and agreeing with them. Several women felt uncomfortable with this idea. When it came to certain issues, they were unsure whether they could accept someone who held an opposing stance. We had lengthy discussions about the importance of separating someone's worth from their views and opinions. I sensed this was necessary groundwork for lasting relationships.

Then came the time Darcy and I went out for Thai food. Darcy loves to talk politics and I'm always looking for common ground in our conversations. Among other things, we both care about education, the environment, and protecting the marginalized. But I remember the moment when she asked me point blank why I was reluctant to "all in" with a political party. We locked eyes and I hesitated. I wondered if our relationship could hold the weight of a conversation soaked in difference. As I shared honestly and vulnerably, her facial expression soften. "I understand," she said. And with that, our friendship went to a whole new level of depth and trust.

I (Chris) had the same opportunity with Ralph. We've collaborated on neighborhood gatherings and events for years and Ralph has become like a brother. We play pickleball when we can, get other neighbors together to play nerdy board games, and stay current with how we're navigating challenges surrounding work and kids. Despite seeing the world through a different lens, we have a lot in common and a high degree of respect for each other. So, a couple years ago, when we both noticed an altercation between some mutual friends on social media over their differing ideologies, Ralph said he wanted to get coffee and chat. "What are your thoughts on all this?" His tone wasn't intense, but the undertone was. Given the heavy nature of the topic and our cultural lack-of-practice in agreeing to disagree, I knew it would require some extra work to shape the kind of wide space we'd need for constructive dialogue. I felt the pressure to get things right and I feared offending my good friend.

But as we talked, it became clear to both of us that we could draw on the many years of previous deposits we'd put in. We stayed engaged, both when our perspectives were shared and when they diverged. This allowed for robust conversation and we both knew our questions weren't merely philosophical; they were personal. When an alternative perspective was offered, neither of us felt threatened because we knew sameness wasn't a prerequisite for friendship.

What happened that day was rare. Not many neighboring relationships have the down-reaching trust and relational bedrock to support conversations like this one. But imagine if they did. What if rather than fight, we found ways to make peace … especially in difference?

Bad Blood

After six beatitudes that didn't make the world's bestsellers list, finally one we can all get behind: *peace.* We give awards for it, sing songs about it, and show symbols that point toward it. Now this is one we can relate to! We long for inner peace, peace of mind, and peace and quiet.

Certainly those on the grassy hill that day were waiting for it. The Jews had a long, unsettled history. Currently, they were living under the Roman ruler, Tiberius, whose version of peacemaking was to make people do what he said. His stepdad was Caesar Augustus, the first of several Roman Emperors, who had instated the Pax Romana, Latin for "Roman Peace." Through military conquest and subjugation, all were required to pledge allegiance to his Roman way or feel Rome's might. The people suffered financial stress and instability from the impossibly high taxes imposed by the Roman reps, and their beliefs and way of living were being challenged on the regular. And before the Romans it had been the Greeks, then the Persians, the Babylonians, the Assyrians … all the way back to the Egyptians.

To say they'd waited an eternity for someone to bring calm to their chaos is an exaggeration, but they had waited roughly fourteen hundred years, so that pretty much counts. Peace had only ever been a blip on their radar and they were holding out hope for the promise of a peacemaking prince whose rule would finally bring them the peace they longed for—in their neighborhoods and in their hearts and minds.

Won't it be great when we take back the crown and we're in charge again?

Our Own Pax Romana

After taking over some brownies and introducing ourselves to Will and his two sons, Hank and Howie, we assumed we might never speak to them again. Will appeared irritated, frosty, and anxious to say goodbye just as soon as we'd said hello. Although our girls then became good friends with his boys and they played together regularly, communication with Will was still sparse, and we got weird vibes. When we saw him at a neighborhood Easter Egg Hunt, we expected things to be awkward, but we went over to chat anyway. We soon sensed from his posture that something had shifted, and he shared that his youngest son, Howie, wasn't feeling well and needed an extended hospital stay for testing. We offered to help with Hank, and he took us up on it.

We got good news that Howie's condition was fully treatable with the right medication. He mended and so did our relationship with his dad. Over the years, Will, Howie and Hank have come to church with us on occasion and we've had lots of meaningful conversations. It's crazy to think that now we share garage codes, carpool, and hang out occasionally—all with someone we previously avoided.

But Will still has a prickly side. He gets going on our neighborhood socials and can be a real pill. We see him unnecessarily provoke and antagonize neighbors and it drives us crazy. If we didn't have that history with him, based on his other behaviors, it'd be easy for us to get sideways. After all, we can choose our friends, doctors, dentists, churches, and the person we marry, but we can't choose our families, or our neighbors. At times we wish we could.

If we could hand-pick the people around us, would we choose like-minded neighbors or contrary ones? If it was up to us, would we prefer that those next-door resembled or were different from us? We can get clues from our phone's contact list and who's present—and absent—at our dinner tables. Who's included—and missing—in our photos? Do the names and faces feel generally similar or dissimilar? We tend to like likeness. After all, we tell ourselves, *blessed are those who seek sameness, for they will never have to resolve conflict with anyone.*

But then our neighborhoods are often mixed bags. They're smorgasbords, jumbled with difference. At times we share proximity with neighbors of different ages, from different cultural backgrounds and socio-economic status, in different life stages, with different personalities, lifestyles, political views, and family structures …

This can make for a beautiful mosaic when neighbors are up for learning from each other, helping one another, and having their assumptions challenged. But at times, we find ourselves wanting our neighbors to see things the way *we* see them, to do things the way *we* do them, and conflict occurs. The fact that we can't choose our neighbors is brought to the forefront, especially when neither of us moves and we're stuck living next to each other … *for years.*

We're triggered when we see our neighbor outside performing a morning religious ritual that's different from ours. Or when we see they have way too many people living under that one roof (*Doesn't that go against the code of conduct?*), rather than respond to these differences with curiosity, we disdain them.

Or it's other things that set us off: their exterior paint color, all the traffic they bring in and out, or the fact that they took our mail by mistake. All of this gets under our skin and we build a case against them.

This is one reason why neighboring can be frustrating for any of us control freaks: we don't get a say. Maybe we wish we could have our own version of a Pax Romana. If we were in charge, it'd be smooth sailing. Our counterfeit beatitude tells us that if we could force conformity, we'd all get along just fine. Life would be so much easier if we could hand-pick our neighbors and how they live. It's hard to imagine making peace with people we wouldn't choose who are just so … different.

This nagging control-loss might tempt us to indulge in some neighborly gossip to rally others to our side. When Donnie next door lets his pet run unleashed or be unruly at 10pm, we see no problem in looking for the power person to help us call the shots. Instead of attempting peacemaking through an in-person conversation, we file a complaint with a governing neighborhood association. If there's no official neighborhood person to hear our protests, we might go to the ultimate authority to pray the neighbors away, asking God to make them disappear altogether.

So, what do we do with the peace gaps? In neighborly conflicts, some of us are fighters, some of us are flighters, and on certain days, we might be a mixture of both. We might become pot-stirrers or conversely, conflict-avoiders—appeasing and accommodating until we're bitter and can hardly hold it in. We default to challenge or tolerance. We're outspoken or won't speak up, we're too blunt or too nice.

Neighboring strikes a nerve because we're just not in control.

The Peacemaking Pathway

God's people, not unlike us, were convinced that peace would flood their hearts once power did. But with this beatitude, Jesus offers a peace that's powerful in a different way. If meekness is the remix of what it means to be poor in spirit, peacemaking is the doppelganger for righteousness; they go together.

> Love and faithfulness meet together; righteousness and peace kiss each other (Ps. 85:10).

Remember, righteousness looks around and seeks to make the wrong things right. It deals with restoring God's design for prosperity and order in our neighborhoods. It desires to see harmony and health come to our communities through doing the right thing. It's acting on an inner hunger for things to be as they ought to be.

James tells us that when we sow this seventh beatitude, we get the fourth: "Peacemakers who sow in peace reap a harvest of righteousness" (Jam. 3:18).

So how are these two co-workers distinct?

Peacemaking is a specific pathway of righteousness that puts things right through restoring relational fractures and conflicts. The peacemaker brings neighbors together—amends are made, tears are repaired, and harmony happens. Things are made good.

To really understand what Jesus meant by peacemaking, we need to understand his view of peace. It's that *shalom* we talked about, the state of neighborhood well-being where all is well. In the second beatitude, it's what we've mourned losing: community wholeness.

Isaiah reminds us that one day, all peace will be restored for those trusting in Jesus. This is what we can invite others into by giving them a small glimpse of that peace now. On that wonderful day, all wrongs will be righted, the lonely will be made unlonely, the wounded healed, and the vulnerable will be made secure. Justice will roll down like waters and righteousness like an ever-flowing stream.

> The wolf will live with the lamb,
>   the leopard will lie down with the goat,
> the calf and the lion and the yearling together;
>   and a little child will lead them.
> The cow will feed with the bear,

> their young will lie down together,
> and the lion will eat straw like the ox.
> The infant will play near the cobra's den,
> and the young child will put its hand into the viper's nest.
> They will neither harm nor destroy
> on all my holy mountain,
> for the earth will be filled with the knowledge of the LORD
> as the waters cover the sea (Is. 11:6–9).

Jesus' peace was and is fundamentally different from the versions of peace our world has to offer. His peace is not a state of mindfulness or a Zen feeling. It's not found in a neighborhood program and doesn't come by taking control. It's not a temporary thing that comes and goes. His peace is a restoring, right-making, reconciling presence, a person: himself. Jesus is our peace.

> I have told you these things, so that *in me* you may have peace. In this world you will have trouble. But take heart! I have overcome the world (Jn. 16:33, emphasis added).

> For *he himself* is our peace (Eph. 2:14, emphasis added).

All our hopes for calm, order, and restoration in our neighborhood conflicts, clashes, and rifts come together in Jesus. Our final answer for harmony, wholeness, and amends in our neighborly disagreements, disputes, and tension is found in Jesus himself.

Weighed and Found Wanting

Jesus is the main ingredient in our neighborhood peacemaking and his way is so different from the world's.

The world's peace can't solve our biggest conflict

History is full of kings and dictators who brutally instituted order at the cost of countless lives. Whereas most empires required allegiance as a prerequisite for peace, Jesus' beatitude-way was propitiatory. He knew our biggest conflict wasn't with Bob next door; our biggest break up was with God himself. When our relationship with our creator wasn't right, Jesus made restitution by offering his own life. When we had bad blood with God, he offered his own as our peace offering.

> … and through him to reconcile to himself all things, whether things on earth or things in heaven, by making peace through his blood, shed on the cross (Col. 1:20).

> Therefore, since we have been justified through faith, we have peace with God through our Lord Jesus Christ (Rom. 5:1).

Jesus graciously gave his life as a gift, knowing we'd fight and flee, nitpick, and distrust, steamroll, and avoid our neighbors, all the while asking, "Why can't we all just get along?" Our prince chose a crown of thorns and extended a peace free-of-charge, but not free for him. His peace is not like the world's.

The world's peace can't calm our current storms

After resolving our biggest conflict on the cross, Jesus didn't just tell us to wait for heaven to enjoy more of the peace we need and crave. In real time, he interrupts our chaos by calming our current storms:

> A furious squall came up, and the waves broke over the boat, so that it was nearly swamped. Jesus was in the stern, sleeping on a cushion. The disciples woke him and said to him, "Teacher, don't you care if we drown?" He got up, rebuked the wind and said to the waves, "Quiet! Be still!" Then the wind died down and it was completely calm. He said to his disciples, "Why are you so afraid? Do you still have no faith?" They were terrified and asked each other, "Who is this? Even the wind and the waves obey him!" (Mk. 4:37–41)

Jesus is not a distant dictator; he moved out of his neighborhood into ours to be near. When we are swayed by stormy seas, he is in the boat. He wants his calm and assurance to shush all the un-peace in our homes and hoods. Jesus offers a deep abiding *shalom* now for us.

The world's peace can't offer future hope

Amidst our messes, Jesus helps us relax by grounding us in his bigger story. He reminds us that though our neighborhoods may be brimming with isolation today, they weren't and won't always be like that. One day, he'll reign, and his permanent peace will be everywhere.

> Then the angel showed me the river of the water of life, as clear as crystal, flowing from the throne of God and of the Lamb down the middle of the great street of the city. On each side of the river stood the tree of life, bearing twelve crops of fruit, yielding its fruit every month. And the leaves of the tree are for the healing of the nations. No longer will there be any curse. The throne of God and of the Lamb will be in the city,

> and his servants will serve him. They will see his face, and his name will be on their foreheads. There will be no more night. They will not need the light of a lamp or the light of the sun, for the Lord God will give them light. And they will reign for ever and ever (Rev. 22:1–5).

Knowing there's a forever peace coming helps us loosen up. What's stressing us out? What are we losing sleep over? What feels like it'll never be okay? Jesus assures us:

> Do not let your hearts be troubled. You believe in God; believe also in me. My Father's house has many rooms; if that were not so, would I have told you that I am going there to prepare a place for you? And if I go and prepare a place for you, I will come back and take you to be with me that you also may be where I am (Jn. 14:1–3).

When we act as neighborhood *shalom*-makers, we give our neighbors glimpses of the permanent peace that's to come.

But even though most of us wouldn't declare we're "at war with the neighbors," next-door conflicts are a common thing and when there's bad blood next door, we need more than a unity service. Unity, while awesome, stops short. It brings neighbors together based on common ground and shared values, but then when it comes to the hard stuff, it leaves unfinished business. Peacemaking doesn't ignore but forgives grievances; it doesn't deny but embraces differences. Peace can be made and sustained when we're willing to move forward with neighbors despite disagreement, dissimilarity, and past disputes.

While the world's peace has been weighed and found wanting, the peace Jesus offers is humble, it is reconciling, it is present, and it is permanent.

It's Messy

Each spring, we gather all the neighbors for a street party. Everyone comes—those who've been around a while and new people, too—young and old. It's a giant potluck where everyone brings food and the kids run around in glorious fashion. With how it's grown over the years, it's become a lot of work, but it's worth it, given that we can trace most relationships back to that gathering.

One year, a few weeks into planning, our neighbors Art and Annie texted to ask if instead of doing a potluck we might use their food truck. We really liked the existing "all participation" aspect of this community-style meal, so it seemed an obvious "no" to me (Elizabeth). Without considering it, I dismissed the idea. Art felt shut down, and he began asking if other neighbors had a preference. Things escalated quickly as we started getting all kinds of texts from neighbors chiming in with their two cents. It felt chaotic and divisive … all over a menu. The food crisis sorted itself out but there was residual frustration between us and Art and Annie, neighbors we'd been close to for many years.

We apologized for being hasty and dismissive, but it was received with a cold shoulder. They expressed their irritation to other neighbors, and we were worried it might never get resolved. We found ourselves praying, "Lord, help" and had the sense that if we were going to make peace, it would be on their terms, so we gave some space. A couple months later when we saw them while walking our dogs, we felt the urge to avoid them. Instead, we walked over and made small talk. It was awkward, but we pushed through. A good two years have passed since it all happened, and we're so thankful to say things have been completely restored.

Neighborhood peacemaking is messy. We also know the turbulence of our own homes, our tendencies to control or avoid, and our pull toward power, rather than love. Lord, help! Just like there's room for our neighbors to make mistakes, there's grace for us to get things wrong, too. We are poor in spirit, inadequate, insufficient.

Thankfully, Jesus is the hero, not us.

Our New Nickname

Our family loves nicknames. We've got Mac, Eliz, Gingey, Pearlie-girl, Juneybug, and Annie Banani. Sometimes you have a say in your nickname and sometimes people pick them for you and you're just stuck with it.

Augustus loved nicknames, too, but he certainly wanted to pick his own. After declaring his deceased dad, Julius, "God" he conveniently had divine association and could start going by "Son of God."[1] Such a powerful title showed he was legit and carried with it a lot of sway. He wanted to be the star of the Pax Romana.

As Jesus' peacemakers, God refers to us in a distinct way: "Blessed are the peacemakers, *for they will be called children of God*" (Mt. 5:9, emphasis added).

This is a title God gives us, not the other way around. Quite the contrast to a star like Augustus, huh? Whereas the other beatitudes promise his kingdom, his comfort, the earth, satisfaction, mercy, and the ability to see God himself, here he gives us a title, a name. He wants his peacemakers to know this is an identifier of what it means to be a child of God.

The promise in Jesus' peacemaking is that he brings together those who would be adversaries and calls them brothers. When we take this desire for reconciliation into our neighborhoods, it reflects that we're his kids. Though God is the name-giver, our family reputation is meant to catch on. Remember how Jesus said, "By this everyone will know that you are my disciples, if you love one another" (Jn. 13:35)? This beatitude gives our neighbors the chance to know we are God's children—when we make peace with one another.

Our neighbors, Leo and Frank, didn't see eye-to-eye. What began as a misunderstanding about property lines grew into a considerable spat, which grew into a full-blown neighborhood feud. We were connected to both, so we tried to serve as mediators when the two went head-to-head. Seeing the way Frank handled things—including his temper and emotional theatrics—I (Chris) started developing my own frustration toward him. I felt sympathetic toward Leo and grudgey toward Frank. I had to decide: How was being a child of the peacemaking God going to affect my feelings toward this neighborly row?

My heart began to soften. I didn't want to stay angry at Frank forever. Leo, on the other hand, made it clear that Frank was pretty much dead to him, and time wouldn't change that. He said he respected my decision to forgive but he never would.

The story isn't finished with Frank and Leo. Neither have expressed much of a spiritual interest up to this point, but I pray that one day, peace will bring them together as brothers who claim the truth of 1 John:

> See what great love the Father has lavished on us, that we should be called children of God! And that is what we are! (1 Jn. 3:1).

Preemptive Peacemaking

We don't have to wait till there's a problem to follow in our Father's footsteps. When it comes to our neighborhoods, how many bad things could be averted by a proactive and preemptive plan for peacemaking, one which involves coming together before things get difficult?

Preemptive peacemaking is a forward-looking approach that seeks to hold off impending neighborhood strife. Contrary to the peacemaking that happens between two warring parties, pre-emptive peacemaking seeks to address potential neighborhood conflicts and cut them off at the pass. It involves proactive cooperation with neighbors of all types to build a neighborhood infrastructure that nurtures safety and security ... *peace*.

This is a wise and prudent kind of neighborhood peace-making. It happens through the collaborative efforts of varied neighbors who team together for the sake of a strong neighborhood whereby residents can be known and grown. These purposeful community-builders know that when the social infrastructure of a neighborhood has been neglected, neighbors become vulnerable to further fray. Through small initiatives and gatherings, neighbors say no to disconnection and emotional distance and become co-creators of flourishing communities where violence is reduced, and tensions are diffused.

What little olive branches could we offer and how might they change someone's day … or eternity? What difference might it make to draw near to neighbors of different worldviews and stun them with the Jesus who pursues them to the farthest belief system? We can dream how it might change things if our spiritually curious neighbors experienced the love of God over them, how they might come to rest in the peace that pursues their heart. We can envision the impact of a peace-giving expression or listening ear when a nearby brother or sister in Christ is deconstructing their faith. We can picture them finding freedom in the peace that keeps them.

What difference would it make in our neighborhoods if we made Jesus' peace with all different kinds of neighbors? It would reflect the beautiful kingdom value of a king who calls his hodgepodge neighbors with all different personalities, from all different neighborhoods, who speak all different languages, with all different skin colors:

> After this I looked, and there before me was a great multitude that no one could count, from every nation, tribe, people and language, standing before the throne and before the Lamb. They were wearing white robes and were holding palm branches in their hands. And they cried out in a loud voice: "Salvation belongs to our God, who sits on the throne, and to the Lamb" (Rev. 7:9–10).

What a beautiful peace Jesus makes.

For Reflection:

"Blessed are the peacemakers, for they will be called children of God."

What do you find most challenging about this invitation to make peace with our neighbors? What do you find most visionary?

Our daily prayer: "Lord, give me courage to make peace with neighbors who are different from me."

Neighbors and situations to pray for this week:

For Discussion:

1. Contrast unity with peacemaking. Share about a personal conflict with a neighbor that needed peace. What happened?
2. Describe preemptive peacemaking and its benefits. What are the barriers or obstacles that hinder us from making this kind of "early" peace in our neighborhoods?
3. Share some differences between you and your neighbors—age, cultural background, socio-economic status, life stages, personality, lifestyle, political views, family structure, or other. What challenges have these differences presented?
4. Compare the peace that Jesus makes with the peace our world offers. As you reflect on Jesus' peacemaking, what motivates you to engage in this important aspect of his mission?
5. How does Jesus value bringing together people who hold conflicting views or who are from diverse backgrounds? (Think about his disciples and see also Revelation 7:9–10.) What practical steps can you take to demonstrate this value in your relationships with both churched and unchurched neighbors?

8

Counting the Cost

Jesus said: "Blessed are those who are persecuted because of righteousness, for theirs is the kingdom of heaven."

The world says: "Blessed are those who fly under the radar, for they will blend right in, and no one will ever suspect they follow King Jesus."

For the last two years, I (Elizabeth) have attended the Bible at the beach retreat in Gulf Shores, Alabama. It's been a wonderful time to get away from the normal responsibilities of life, reflect and walk by the ocean, hear good teaching, and eat lots of raw oysters. In 2022, Nancy Guthrie did a deep dive into the often-avoided New Testament book of Revelation, you know, a light and easy beach read. I was amazed at how my initial feelings of intimidation were transformed into awe and worship. For the first time, Revelation was demystified as Nancy persuaded us that this book is not about unscrambling some secret code or trying to crunch and match numbers with current events, rather that it offers eternal perspective to ordinary believers like you and me. She said Revelation was meant to "jolt us out of our complacency … and to change how we feel, what we fear and what we want."[1]

It seems easier when we encounter difficult Scripture passages to either jump in with our calculators and code-crackers or prematurely assign a meaning that's not there. It's much harder and scarier to sit in a passage and open ourselves to what is already clear. It's just too uncomfortable.

I wonder if that's how some of us feel about this last beatitude. No matter how many times we keep running the numbers, trying to unscramble what Jesus might have meant by "blessed are the persecuted," we keep getting the same difficult answer: there's a cost to following King Jesus.

Because of Me

Open Doors, an organization dedicated to supporting the persecuted church, reports that right now there are more than 360 million Christians worldwide—one in seven—who suffer high levels of persecution and discrimination for their faith. This includes believers discovered in North Korean house churches who—if spared—are sent as political prisoners to labor camps. It involves Muslims who've turned to Jesus in Afghanistan but remain in hiding from Taliban extremists who search door-to-door to kill anyone considered an apostate. It refers to believing women in Sub-Saharan Africa who are targeted for sexual attack. It includes Christians in China who are "branded 'troublemakers', 'disturbers of the peace' or even 'terrorists'" for their refusal to support the ruling party.[2] They face arrest, and worse.

The book of Hebrews described such troublemakers:

> There were others who were tortured, refusing to be released so that they might gain an even better resurrection. Some faced jeers and flogging, and even chains and imprisonment. They were put to death by stoning; they were sawed in two; they were killed by the sword … the world was not worthy of them (Heb. 11:35–38).

This eighth and final call to flourishing is an invitation to share in Jesus' sufferings, specifically the injuries of enmity. It is, in the words of Dietrich Bonhoeffer, "the bid to come and die."

Let's be honest: it feels like Jesus saved the worst beatitude for last. It's emotionally difficult to think about someone being persecuted for their faith. It's upsetting to learn about the abuse of power that occurs around the world, denying dignity to our brothers and sisters in Christ. It's uncomfortable to confront our own views of suffering and expectations for the Christian life. And it can cause us to call into question our own capacity to endure such hardship and to ask why God would allow his people to suffer such brutality.

And yet, Jesus wants our hearts to be moved and challenged by the courage and cost of those who are living faithfully for Jesus. And to go further, he wants to prepare us for our own experience of it: "Remember what I told you: 'A servant is not greater than his master.' If they persecuted me, they will persecute you also" (Jn. 15:20). Paul delivers the ultimate blow: "In fact, *everyone* who wants to live a godly life in Christ Jesus will be persecuted" (2 Tim. 3:12, emphasis added).

By everyone, does Paul really *mean … everyone?*

Jesus highlights that persecution can come in different forms, including insults and untruths, but either way, these oppressive behaviors aren't random acts of cruelty. He explains the reason for such severity in his next sentence in Matthew 5: "Blessed are you when people insult you, persecute you and falsely say all kinds of evil against you *because of me*" (Mt. 5:11, emphasis added).

Jesus goes out of his way to clarify that persecution comes "because of righteousness" and "because of me," not because of our particular politics, our fanatical faith, or our brash personality.[3] This mistreatment excludes ordinary setbacks and challenges, criticism for overzealousness, or just being the neighborhood moron.[4] Instead it has to do with a refusal to compromise your deep commitment to God, the resisting of temptation to go against your personal convictions, confronting unjust leaders, sharing your faith, and other instances of openly worshiping and following Jesus.

In essence, persecution is the attempt to displace and drive out the presence of Christ's kingdom through hostile and adversarial acts. It is a punishment that comes as a direct result of a Christian's bold allegiance to him. In neighborly terms, it is the attempt to evict Jesus and his followers from the neighborhood.

From the Margins

Our friends, Mandy and Mark, had been building relationships with their neighbors over several years, hosting small Sunday sushi nights and fondue parties, as well as neighborhood book discussions consisting of books written by Christian authors on topics like marriage and parenting. This all came to a screeching halt when their neighbor, Anita, had a bone to pick. While their kids were playing together, Anita asked some probing questions about the books Mandy had chosen for her book club. Her tone cold and hard, she expressed that Mandy should be more open-minded, insisting that Christianity itself was dogmatic and unsafe.

After this, Mandy overheard Anita and some other neighbors blatantly talking about her at the bus stop, not far away. Neighbors with whom she'd previously shared a tuna roll, now moved across to the opposite sidewalk. The neighborhood text thread grew quiet, and she realized a new one had been formed. She began to dread the thought of dropping her kids off in the morning, and she felt anxious, sad, and uninvited.

Another friend, Adrien, lives in a neighborhood in Marseille, France. He was recently describing some of the challenges to following Christ in his corner of Western Europe and illustrated his point with a story about his neighbor and running buddy, Felix. Adrien noticed that around Christmastime, Felix began to post antagonizing memes about Jesus and Christianity. Adrien wasn't sure what to make of it but hoped he'd have the chance to hear the backstory at some point. Unfortunately, he didn't have the chance. As soon as Felix realized that Adrien was a believer, an awkward tension developed, and he began to distance himself.

For some, the opposition they face for being a Christian can be severe, for others, more subtle. But big or small, the resistance that comes from hitching our wagons to Jesus takes a toll. Many, like Mandy and Adrien, find there is a marginalization that awaits Jesus' followers and it's not for the faint of heart. Marginalization happens when your voice is silenced or quieted, and your place of power is removed or relegated to the edges of the neighborhood. It's a muting and an ousting, like an assigned laryngitis to deny your influence and importance. Its intention is to send you packing.

Blessed are you when people insult you. Whether to our face or behind our back, we need not be surprised when we're demeaned, slighted, patronized, criticized, or gossiped about by neighbors who have an intolerance toward Christianity. Woe to you if all neighbors speak well of you.

Blessed are you when people persecute you. It's much more fun to be in the center of the circle and can really hurt to be sidelined, snubbed, and canceled. When neighbors find out we're with Jesus, we might be edged and left out, or even blocked. In a very real sense, we'll feel like spiritual refugees.

Blessed are you when people falsely say all kinds of evil against you. Jesus is clear that there will come a time when neighbors make snap judgments and false assumptions about us. We'll feel misrepresented, disparaged, and potentially vilified.

Behind the Curtain

We might initially scan over the "enemy" verses of Matthew 5:10–12 because, well, it's all a bit intense this talk of having enemies … until the times we feel really attacked and angry and unjustly judged; then we're thankful to be able to name it as it is.

Jesus didn't hesitate to acknowledge that he had adversaries, even spiritual ones. Whereas it might be odd for some to subscribe to the supernatural, Jesus was quite familiar with the unseen realm. He knew there was a whole cast of characters at work behind the scenes and that our true enemies weren't each other, rather the rebellious spiritual beings that seek to inspire "hatred, division, and violence."[5]

Paul concurred: "For our struggle is not against flesh and blood, but against the rulers, against the authorities, against the powers of this dark world and against the spiritual forces of evil in the heavenly realms" (Eph. 6:12).

When we partner with God to see his kingdom values occupy our neighborhoods, we can be sure that there is a whole hidden dimension of spiritual beings who are working toward the opposite ends. These undercover renegades seek to animate behind the curtain, to galvanize a rebellion against the very meekness, mercy, and peace God is calling us to sow. They incite disorder, doom, and contempt because the neighborhoods they reimagine are filled with the anti-*shalom*.

It's important to remember this as we encounter resistance to Jesus' beatitude-way. When it comes to neighboring, there's more going on than meets the eye. When our neighbor's tendency is to dehumanize us or show a caustic attitude toward us for our faith, we can recognize that there's activity in the wings and backstage. When we're sent to the social fringes or our neighbors project unjust prejudices upon us for our faithful witness, we understand our struggle is not against flesh and blood.

This changes the way we view our neighbors. Rather than merely see a bully, we start to see an image-bearer. We maintain boundaries when necessary but also discover empathy. Our hearts soften and so do our prayers.

Our adversarial neighbors are not our true adversaries.

Under the Radar

As this portion of the Sermon on the Mount wraps up, some of us are pulling out our expense reports wondering how much Jesus wants from us. Weighing the pros-and-cons, we ask, *Is the kind of flourishing Jesus promises really worth the cost?*

Peter had his doubts. We might have thought that, as one of Jesus' closest followers, surely he would've been willing to put his neck on the line for the one he called, "Messiah, the Son of the Living God" (Mt. 16:16). He got there, but it took him a while.

We can't help but speculate what was going on in Peter's mind when he first heard Jesus list all these beatitude rewards. He was presumably gung-ho for the previous blessings, but we wonder what his thoughts were regarding the final persecution award. He presented unwavering self-confidence when it came to his commitment to Christ: "Even if all fall away on account of you, I never will … Even if I have to die with you, I will never disown you" (Mt. 26:33, 35). But then just a few verses later, when push came to shove, he's swearing up and down and pinky-promising servant girls that he's never seen the guy before in his life. A few bystanders ask about their association, and he tries to blend in with the wallpaper: *Never heard of him.*

He wasn't the only one: "Yet at the same time many even among the leaders believed in him. But because of the Pharisees they would not openly acknowledge their faith for fear they would be put out of the synagogue; for they loved human praise more than praise from God" (Jn. 12:42–43).

It's easy to be a critic when we read passages like these, but are we really much different? In these instances, some didn't want to go public with Jesus because they were afraid of the mob mentality, so they played it safe. Do we do the same? Do we love human praise and fear the consequences of running in Jesus' circle? When the chips are down, do we go hush-hush and dissociate from Jesus, so we don't look like the bad guy? Do we know how to be in the world but not of the world, or are we afraid to put all our eggs in Jesus' basket? Do we know when to blend in and when to stand out?

Jesus prayed for his followers, not that we'd be taken out of the world but that we'd be protected from the evil one (Jn. 17:15). In every time and culture, there have been good, God-honoring ways for his people to assimilate into their neighborhoods. But there are ways in which we shouldn't fit, too. Paul says: "Do not conform to the pattern of this world, but be transformed by the renewing of your mind. Then you will be able to test and approve what God's will is—his good, pleasing and perfect will" (Rom. 12:2). Rather than looking just like the world and following the patterns and programs all the other neighbors are using, we're to be changed by this beatitude template:

> In self-sufficient neighborhoods, we're called to be poor in spirit.
> In numbed-out neighborhoods, we're called to mourn.
> In me-first neighborhoods, we're called to meekness.
> In soul-starved neighborhoods, we're called to righteousness.
> In karma-driven neighborhoods, we're called to mercy.
> In hypocritical neighborhoods, we're called to be pure in heart.
> In contentious neighborhoods, we're called to make peace.

And in neighborhoods where it's cost-prohibitive to follow Jesus, the first seven will have shaped and prepared us for the test of persecution.

This undesirable invitation is not reserved for flawless followers but is outstretched to all us Peters out there who've at times been sheepish about our friendship with Jesus. It's a call to those of us who've wondered if the cost is really worth it, who've felt ashamed or apathetic or sleepy in our faith, who've feared rejection and whose faith has felt frail. Sometimes Jesus mercifully sounds the crow of a rooster to change how we feel, what we fear, what we want, and to remind us of who we really are; then welcomes us back with open arms (Jn. 21:15–19).

Aren't we thankful that this teacher who offers classes in persecution is the same who offers mercy? Jesus didn't give up on his fair-weather friend and he forgives and keeps us when we're too embarrassed to admit that he's ours.

Uno Reverse

In some ways, Jesus looked a lot like his next-door neighbors. He used the same spice rub on his rack of lamb, wore the same tunic and Birkenstocks that his friends did, spoke in Aramaic, told stories, played games, celebrated all the holidays and festivals, went to synagogue and paid taxes. But then there were other ways in which he broke the social norms and was the odd one out, eating with sinners and tax collectors, engaging with the unwanted and eventually being charged as a criminal. He knew when to go with the flow and when to break the mold.

We prefer being popular to being on the periphery, but Jesus didn't; he came straight to the margins. Margins were among many things Jesus wasn't intimidated by, like false accusations, bullies, and associating with the wrong people. Jesus was quite comfortable on the hem.

His ministry grew that way, with outcasts on the outskirts of the neighborhood, challenging the mainstream way of thinking. He stood up to the spiritual powers and authorities, going toe-to-toe with shadowy spirits who'd been working to ensnare and subdue the vulnerable. He exposed the dark hold they had on neighbors and the violence they inspired. And he sought to reclaim and restore *shalom* to every neighborhood, from every spiritual rebel who fought to destroy it.

The spiritual powers didn't like this so much and tried hard to discredit, displace, and ultimately dethrone him. So, when Jesus offered up this last beatitude, he wasn't asking his followers to go through anything he himself wasn't willing to endure. By the end of his life, he was all too acquainted with persecution, including the forms he said we'd face—criticism, exclusion, and accusation—but others, too.

Imagine the Son of God criticized for not washing his hands (Mk. 7:5) and insulted for running with the wrong crowd (Lk. 15:2). Imagine the lack of welcome he felt in his hometown (Lk. 4:24). To say they were trying to get rid of him is an understatement—they tried to throw him off a cliff (Lk. 4:29)! Political and religious leaders, everyday neighbors, and even his own family believed all kinds of nasty things about him circulated by his unseen enemies in the rumor mill—including that he was crazy (Mk. 3:21), blasphemous (Mk. 2:7), demon-possessed (Jn. 8:48), and an over-eater and a drunk (Mt. 11:19). Judas and Peter betrayed him, and when he was arrested, *all* his friends left him (Mt. 26:56). And as the ultimate spoof, he was pageanted with a crown, regal robes and royal sign above his head, with nearby scoffers hailing and kneeling sarcastically, before he was stripped (Mk. 15:17–20; 26). These persecutions were verbal, physiological, social, and all very real.

Then there was the unthinkable physical abuse that Jesus suffered. If there was ever a thought that the gates of hell could prevail against God's church, it came when Jesus was betrayed, arrested, spat on, struck, and beaten (Mt. 26:47, 67). He was made to carry a heavy, wooden crossbeam through the streets toward Calvary and then nails were driven through his hands and feet (Mt. 27:32–35). It wasn't until they heard Jesus pray to God and ask why he'd been forsaken that they finally spoke of leaving him alone (Mk. 15:34–36).

But the gates of hell didn't prevail. With the ultimate Uno Reverse card, Jesus punked his enemies. What appeared as ultimate defeat, was ironically God's plan from the beginning, his very means of confronting and disarming the rebel authorities. What they intended as the greatest act of evil, Jesus accomplished as the greatest act of love, willingly taking sin's scorn and shame upon himself, and enduring the wrath of God on our behalf. Right there in the afternoon darkness, the earth shook, rocks split, and tombs opened; Jesus silenced the powers of darkness by demonstrating his divinity and rising from the dead (Mt. 27:51–52). God's people were expecting military conquest and the lion of God but what they got was a slain, blood-soaked Lamb. This was how the kingdom of heaven was inaugurated, in Jesus' promise to overcome his enemies through sacrifice and love.[6]

Snapshot

If our muscles are stiff from inflammation, we get a massage and take some ibuprofen. If our dough is tough, we add some liquid and let it rest. If the soil in our garden is hard, we add compost, till and water it. But when a neighbor's heart is hard, what do we do?

Christians in Jerusalem and surrounding areas avoided Saul, whose heart was so hard he wreaked havoc, going door-to-door breathing murderous threats and arresting anyone who associated with Jesus (Acts 9:1–2; 21). He proudly and callously gave approval for the stoning of Stephen, whose focus was distributing food to Greek-speaking Jewish-Christian widows before he became the first martyr (Acts 6:1–6; 8:1). Never in a million years would Saul have foreseen himself enduring for Jesus the same kind of persecution that he had inflicted on others. Yet, Jesus came to him on the road of Damascus, saying he took these persecutions personally, and next thing you know, Saul made a 180, changed his name, was baptized, and began to persuade anyone he could that the one he once persecuted was now worthy of anything it cost him.

Saul—better known as the New Testament writer Paul—was later beaten with rods, pelted with stones, lashed, and chased (2 Cor. 11:23–26); the one who'd been mistreating, vilifying, and pushing out, was now the mistreated, vilified, and pushed. So, what changed? How did the persecutor become the persecuted?

Paul later writes: "do you show contempt for the riches of his kindness, forbearance and patience, not realizing that *God's kindness* is intended to lead you to repentance?" (Rom. 2:4, emphasis added).

God's kindness changed his hard heart. God's transformative work caused him to consider everything else in his life as garbage, compared to knowing Christ and sharing in his sufferings (Phil. 3:8, 10). As impossible as it would have seemed to any neighboring onlookers, Jesus got the best of this obstinate adversary, not with the law or with a sword, but by lovingly laying down his own life as a sacrifice for him.

We can win our neighbors this way, too, even the ones who are hard to love.

We don't have a ton of enemies in our neighborhood but I'm sure there are neighbors who don't like us. There's Jack, who we can't say has sidelined us for our faith specifically, but for years has been cold, critical, and combative toward us. If we had to pick an enemy, it'd be him. And Gretchen. She's another hard one—belligerent, demeaning, condescending … They happen to be married to each other. It's hard to imagine Jack and Gretchen ever softening to the gospel, much less preaching and living it. We know it's not good to hate them back, but what about a very strong dislike?

> You have heard that it was said, "Love your neighbor and hate your enemy." But I tell you, love your enemies and pray for those who persecute you (Mt. 5:43–44).

We can love and pray for unlikeable neighbors by faith while we ask God to help our emotions catch up. However, what do we do when it's worse than this? How can we sustain our efforts to love someone whose aim is to hurt us or to drive us out? How did Paul do it when he was the one being evicted? What grounded him to be able to love those who wanted the worst for him?

> Who shall separate us from the love of Christ? Shall trouble or hardship or persecution or famine or nakedness or danger or sword? … No, in all these things we are more than conquerors through him who loved us. For I am convinced that neither death nor life, neither angels nor demons, neither the present nor the future, nor any powers, neither height nor depth, nor anything else in all creation, will be able to separate us from the love of God that is in Christ Jesus our Lord (Rom. 8:35, 37–39).

God's love secures and enables us to love the people in our surroundings who don't want to see his kingdom come. It enabled Paul to say from personal experience: "Bless those who persecute you; bless and do not curse" (Rom. 12:14). He was able to pray for those who persecuted him and bless them, wanting the best for them, because he knew the sacrificial love of a God who came near to him when he was the enemy. He was able to see Christ-following potential in the most unlikely of neighbors because he was himself an unlikely. We all are.

Rather than wanting the worst for neighbors like Jack and Gretchen, and Anita and Felix, we can remember that they aren't our true enemies at all, and that we serve a God who turns persecutors into preachers. Jesus reminds us here to bless our neighbors and to pray that God will work in their lives like how he's worked in ours.

There are many ways we can bless our antagonistic neighbors but one in particular is to show them something called unconditional positive regard,[7] which essentially means "believing the best about them." It sounds crazy but amidst opposition, we can still refrain from "suspicion, believing the worst, criticism, napping, or blame,"[8] and instead offer acceptance, respect, and empathy. It's not to say we're naïve; we still use caution and common sense. But we don't quiet quit or take up arms against neighbors who are belligerent.

We only have the snapshot; thankfully God has the big picture.

Bookended Blessings

So, did Jesus save the worst beatitude for last, after all? Is it really possible to flourish in the face of opposition? Is the reward for following him worth the cost?

Jesus didn't leave us hanging: "Rejoice and be glad, because great is your reward in heaven, for in the same way they persecuted the prophets who were before you" (Mt. 5:12).

If our neighboring stories ended with us being forever exiles, forever defeated with our forever hurts, we wouldn't have hope to persevere. But that's not our story. We can flourish and have joy now because our defeats are temporary. This is why Paul could belt out his favorite worship songs at midnight from a prison cell and why Jesus could carry his cross (Acts 16:25; Heb. 12:2). Rather than choose retaliation, denial, blame, or something else, they had a rare and mystifying joy. The gladness they had was not an enjoyment of their abuse and did not diminish the realities of their suffering; it was an outward expression of their inner hope. They were emboldened by the many before them who'd shown great endurance in opposition—like Gideon, Barak, Samson, Jephthah, David, and Samuel—whose weakness had turned to strength (Heb. 11:32, 34). They knew relief was coming, and more than that, reward: "for theirs is the kingdom of heaven" (Mt. 5:10).

Despite our initial resistance to Jesus' upside-down way and first impression that these invitations are an underwhelming way to live, we now realize Jesus' leadership isn't the clunky, snoozable style we suspected. For the first time in the beatitudes, Jesus changes his language from general to specific—from blessed are *the* meek and *the* peacemakers ... to blessed are *you*—and, noticing this, we can't help but feel we've underestimated this whole thing (Mt. 5:11–12). We are now face-to-face with the Lamb who was persecuted on our behalf, and the question is this: *What are* you *willing to risk for* him?

For those of us who've never had our heart rates or our blood pressure go up for fear of being found with Jesus, we can be thankful for a favor-filled season with our neighbors and certainly shouldn't go looking for opposition. But we might do well to ask if we've gone far enough. If we've never talked about what Jesus means to us or spoken up on his behalf, we might be too afraid of those who can kill the body but cannot kill the soul (Mt. 10:28). Let's remember Jesus promises to be worthy of any and every cost, guaranteeing us great reward and the kingdom of heaven.

And let's not overlook the connection Jesus is drawing between his first and final beatitude. He first promises the kingdom of heaven will be extended to the poor in spirit and now we find the very same promise for those persecuted for his sake, like "bookended blessings."[9] It's like one big ol' beatitude sandwich. The middle six beatitudes are what's between the bread, pictures of the kingdom itself: comfort and neighborhood *shalom* filling the new earth, God's people fully satisfied by doing his work, mercy abounding, and everyone in God's family seeing his face. By bookending his teaching, Jesus belabors his point: *The one who receives these invitations will see my kingdom come very near and this is what it will look like.*

It's no coincidence that Jesus promised the breaking in of his kingdom specifically for the poor in spirit and the persecuted. He begins and ends with a cost. We begin by emptying our pockets of anything we thought we could offer and cashing in on what Jesus has to offer us instead. As we mourn, and are meek and merciful, we stop believing the promises of our world's counterfeit kingdom. We see through our me-first, Me Monsters who just want to keep score, numb out with me-time, and hide the real us. We no longer believe our culture's version of blessing through independent and comfortable lives where we get what we feel we deserve now.

We come to believe that whatever counterfeit good life the world offers us—with all its achievements, possessions, power, and approval—will pale in comparison to this upside-down kingdom. From the first to the last, the beatitudes show us that yes, following Jesus costs us everything.

But looking back, we had nothing to lose and everything to gain.

For Reflection:

"Blessed are those who are persecuted because of righteousness, for theirs is the kingdom of heaven."

What would be the worst-case scenario for how you imagine this beatitude playing out in your neighborhood? What about the best-case?

Our daily prayer: "Jesus, following you is worth any cost. Bless my neighbors who don't yet know you."

Neighbors and situations to pray for this week:

For Discussion

1. What are some potential reactions we might have to this final beatitude and why? What is Jesus telling us by including the phrase "because of righteousness" or "because of me"?
2. Compare and contrast persecution and marginalization for one's faith. How might God use these experiences to shape how we feel, what we fear, and what we want?
3. Name a time when you wanted to fly under the radar when it came to your faith. What's one takeaway you have from this chapter that speaks into that experience?
4. How does Paul's transformation give you a vision for how God might work in a hostile neighbor's heart?
5. Of the counterfeit beatitudes, which do you most identify with and why?
6. Thinking back on all eight beatitudes, how has your mindset changed toward your neighbors? Pick one specific mindset change to share. What is one practical way you can apply what you've learned?

CONCLUSION

Beatitude Recap

There are two types of families you can marry into: those who do holiday walks and runs, and those who don't. Thankfully for Chris, he married into one that does.

Rather than keep the fun to ourselves, we decided to start a neighborhood "Turkey Trot" on Thanksgiving Day where neighbors could gather to do a mile loop around the neighborhood before stuffing themselves with turkey and other holiday dishes. There's not much to the event itself—we just provide some donuts and hot chocolate and then we walk. But last year, I (Elizabeth) thought maybe we could have some neighbors donate some pies to give away.

I sent an email out to all our residents with my pie idea and soon I heard back from two ladies, Edith and Ruth. I already knew Ruth but had never met seventy-something-year-old Edith. When she called me on the phone to introduce herself and chat details, she went on to tell me all about her estranged relationships with her adult children and recent knee surgery. She said she was hoping to meet some other neighbors so she wouldn't be so alone.

I had Chris's voice in my head: "You've heard it said, 'Bake a pie for your neighbors' but I say bake a pie *with* your neighbors." I asked if she'd be willing to make a pie with our other neighbor, Ruth, and she eagerly agreed. I hoped it would be a match made in heaven.

A week later, Ruth and Edith showed up together at our doorstep with pies for days: chocolate pie, coconut and banana cream, cherry, pecan, and key lime. Edith was beaming. Ruth called me later and told me all about their conversations and how Edith was coming to church with her on Sunday. "I've been praying for ten years that God would use me in this neighborhood to lead someone to Christ. Maybe it's Edith."

Salt Block

Like Ruth and probably you too, we sometimes question how God could ever use people as ordinary as us to accomplish his good purposes and draw others to him.

But ordinary isn't a problem for God. Salt and light might strike us as fairly ordinary too and yet, those are the very metaphors Jesus gives for making a difference in our corners. Remember:

> You are the salt of the earth. But if the salt loses its saltiness, how can it be made salty again? It is no longer good for anything, except to be thrown out and trampled underfoot.
>
> You are the light of the world. A town built on a hill cannot be hidden. Neither do people light a lamp and put it under a bowl. Instead, they put it on its stand, and it gives light to everyone in the house. In the same way, let your light shine before others, that they may see your good deeds and glorify your Father in heaven (Mt. 5:13–16).

Here Jesus connects our character—rather than extraordinary talents—to the mission. It's not about our stunning abilities or super creativeness. It's not about being incredibly eloquent, or mega smart. With no pretense for perfection, Jesus wants us to know that who we are and the way we live matters far more. Rather than be useless, we're to be active and effective. Rather than be hidden, we're to be visible and public. Our flourishing isn't meant to remain unpublished; it's meant to circulate through our subdivisions. These invitations from Jesus are meant to be shared and spread; they're for our neighbors, too.[1]

Without needing to travel overseas or across town, we can help our neighbors see and savor Jesus amidst their bland and dark newsfeeds. In all our ordinariness, we are exactly the salt and the light they need.

The CliffsNotes

You've got to love CliffsNotes—easing millions of students through their Shakespeare coursework and Spanish exams for over sixty years. You'll be relieved to know there's no test coming at the end of this book, but a little recap might help to bring the last eight chapters together, seeing how Jesus' upside-down beatitudes merge into one beautiful vision for our neighborhoods.

First, we spent time thinking about how God might change us and our neighborhoods if we redefined our view of the good life and what it means to be "blessed." We rethought our view of flourishing through this countercultural lens. We realized we can't keep thinking that meekness is loser language or that we must be similar to those around us to make a difference. We need to know mercy firsthand if we're going to show it to a merciless world.

Amidst the divisiveness around us, we discovered the refreshing breeze of the beatitudes. We wondered what it could look like if our lives were transformed by these contrasting values. What if as believers—rather than mirroring the world—our character was connected to the mission? Rather than striving to be rule-followers or merely set good examples, what if our neighbors saw that as Christ-followers, our lives pointed to him?

Without minimizing our need to apply these twelve verses with our friends, families, and every neighbor we pass or with whom we share some kind of space—whether familial, virtual, or physical—we zoomed in on the shared space of physical proximity, the one with our next-door neighbors. As we did, we realized we don't have to travel far to engage in God's mission; we can see God use us right where we are.

We saw that Jesus' promises are in some ways delayed and in other ways for now, so we engaged our missional imaginations to wonder what it might look like for his kingdom to break in and turn our streets right-side-up. The Gospel stories of Jesus healing ears and eyes and withered hands and backs gave us a vision of his curse-canceling power. We dreamt about what our neighborhood could look like if his kingdom were to come, and his will be done now as it is in heaven. We imagined him healing and reversing injustice, addiction, violence, loneliness, family dysfunction, prejudice, and spiritual blindness. These hope-bearing images brought waves of joy and vision for how we might engage in God's mission in new ways. It motivated us to think that who we are and what we do matters to the mission.

It wasn't all sunshine and rainbows, though. The more we understood the meaning of each beatitude, the more we saw our false versions of them, our tendencies to find flourishing our own way. Our hearts were broken. We realized we're unable to live any of these without his help. With each one, we saw ourselves as a dead end and realized this was part of the re-shaping.

Then Jesus. Seeing the ways in which he perfectly fulfilled each beatitude not only deepened our love for him, but instilled a sense of awe. We have a clearer picture now of the kind of future King Jesus will be, one who governs with righteousness, mercy, and peace.

Each beatitude was a journey itself. It was evident that Jesus intended to shrink our self-importance and grow our view of God. At first, our inadequacies and neediness made us cringe. But then we watched Jesus rely on the Father for everything, realized we'll always be spiritual dependents, and started to say, "Lord help!" With mourning, he led us into the foreboding basement elevator, where he demonstrated good grief by surfacing his deep-down emotions. We left with a vision for how his comfort and soothing might transform us into those who comfort and soothe.

Next, we went from me-ness to meekness when we saw Jesus stoop to our level. When he assured us of a future inheritance, we updated our view of prosperity theology and concluded we don't need "our best lives now" because a future award awaits us. This freed us to delay our demands, slow down with our neighbors, and consider going second. From there, Jesus revised our view of righteousness by demonstrating what it looks like to be satisfied by putting things right. We realized that our idols of autonomy and me-time were starving our souls because we were created to be satisfied by doing God's will. So, we rolled up our sleeves and our tastes began to change when we no longer saw our neighborhoods as a drive-thru.

Half-way through, mercy interrupted things. Our inner Pharisee was disarmed when the research revealed we had bad instincts; revenge isn't rewarding after all. In exchange for our moralism, Jesus offered his compounding cycle of compassion, a mercy which meets needs and makes amends. Then came his flourishing for those with whole hearts. We marveled at how Jesus' public and private personas were always the same and how he used his art of repair to fuse our fractured hearts together. This is where our paradigms really flipped, when we stopped hiding our imperfections and saw beauty in our brokenness. We imagined how our own hope for wholeness might remind our neighbors that they're works in progress, too. Where there was bad blood in our neighborhood, Jesus paraded a peace that was different from the world's, an understated but powerful peace that turned rivals into brothers. Rather than keep it private, we imagined publishing this kind of peace in our corners and the difference it could make.

Finally, we recognized that we have unseen opponents who do not want Jesus' kingdom to come to our neighborhoods; they want him evicted. When we tried to fly under the radar with Peter, Jesus wooed us to count the cost of being his. We found comfort in Paul's story, knowing that our neighbors are not the enemy. Rather than demonize them, we can anchor ourselves in God's love to bless and pray for them, knowing we only have the snapshot, not the whole picture.

Who would've thought we could find flourishing this way? Not us, that's for sure. We wouldn't and couldn't have made up a story like this. But Jesus loves an unexpected twist, the kind where skeptics become saltshakers and the leery become light-bearers. It's that Uno Reverse card we don't see coming.

How could the beatitudes turn your neighborhood upside-down? Just imagine.

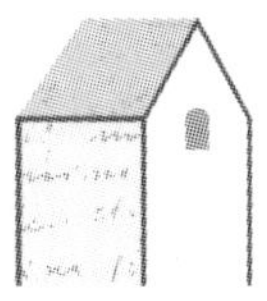

Acknowledgments

Our neighbors: Eleven years ago, our lives were changed when we moved into our neighborhood. Never in a trillion years could we have expected how our lives would be enriched and what God would have planned from that first fish fry. Thanks for jumping in and making WR a fantastic place to live. We love living here with you.

Our ministry partners: This book would not be possible without you. Every conversation that comes, every light bulb that goes off, every heart that shifts—it's because of your faithful and generous giving.

FamilyLife and 10Publishing: Stephen, two years ago, God providentially sat us next to each other while eating pumpernickel "mushroom soil" and miracle berries. We're so glad he did. We've loved working with you and have been so grateful to have had you as our spokesperson. Margie, Tonya, and Ryan, what a gift to pray, share, dream, and learn alongside you three in this shared space. Thank you, Jonathan, Jonathan, Lois, and everyone at 10Publishing who believed in this project and made it happen. And Jude, we love the cover! Perhaps most of all, we owe Sheri a tremendous debt for knowing when and where to focus, delete, reorder, and polish up all our words. You are truly brilliant!

Our friends and co-workers: Kerry, the only gift better than having you for a boss is having you for a friend. We are immeasurably thankful for all your support and encouragement. Rick and Lisa, we're YOUR groupies. Ryan and Kelley, you're the real deal and we love being on a team with you. Your shepherding, wise hearts have helped sustain us in all these years of ministry. Jeremy, you took a chance on us three years ago and there's no way to overstate the significance of your role in discipling us as new authors. We'll always be grateful for you.

Our kids: Ginger, Pearl, June, and Annie: Remember how you prayed this book into existence and then made us promise to do a YES DAY to celebrate? Maybe we should do that every time?! You're forever our four favorite neighbors. And to the rest of our families, we love you tons. We are so thankful for the stories of mercy God has written into our families.

Each other: We did it. We made it to June 1 and we still like each other. Let's do it again sometime.

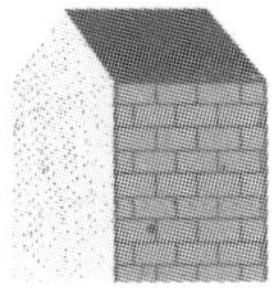

Endnotes

Introduction

1. Howard, Marc M., James L. Gibson, and Dietlend Stolle, *The U.S. Citizenship, Involvement, Democracy Survey*, Center for Democracy and Civil Society (CDACS) (Georgetown University, 2005), 7.
2. Davis, Leslie, and Kim Parker, "A half-century after 'Mister Rogers' debut, 5 facts about neighbors in U.S.," *Pew Research Center* (August 15, 2019). Available at: https://www.pewresearch.org/fact-tank/2019/08/15/ facts-about-neighbors-in-u-s/.
3. Gao, George, "Americans divided on how much they trust their neighbors," *Pew Research Center* (April 13, 2016). Available at: https://www.pewresearch.org/fact-tank/2016/04/13 / americans-divided-on-how-much-they-trust-their-neighbors/.
4. Chua, Amy, and Jed Rubenfeld, "The Threat of Tribalism," *The Atlantic* (October 2018). Available at: https://www.theatlantic.com/magazine/archive/2018/10/the-threat-of-tribalism/568342/.
5. France, R.T., *The Gospel of Matthew*, The New International Commentary on the New Testament (Eerdmans, 2007), 11.
6. Allison, Dale C., *The Sermon on the Mount: Inspiring the Moral Imagination* (Herder & Herder, 1999), 43.
7. Pennington, Jonathan T., *The Sermon on the Mount and Human Flourishing: A Theological Commentary* (Baker Academic, 2017), 26.
8. Ibid., 57, 154.
9. McKnight, Scot, *The Sermon on the Mount*, The Story of God Bible Commentary (Zondervan, 2013), 34.

10. Pennington, Jonathan T., *The Sermon on the Mount and Human Flourishing: A Theological Commentary* (Baker Academic, 2017), 57, 154.
11. This "aha moment" came from reading Jonathan Pennington's thoughts on spreading this flourishing in his book, *The Sermon on the Mount and Human Flourishing: A Theological Commentary* (Baker Academic, 2017), 119.

Chapter 1

1. Toplady, Augustus M., "Rock of Ages," *The United Methodist Hymnal* (The United Methodist Publishing House, 1989), #361.
2. Regan, B., *I Walked On the Moon* [DVD] (Paramount Home Entertainment, 2004).
3. Lloyd-Jones, Martyn, *Studies in the Sermon on the Mount* (Eerdmans Publishing, 1976).
4. Ibid., 27.
5. Wolfgang, P. D. (Director), *The NeverEnding Story* (Bavaria Film, 1984).
6. Murray, Andrew, *Humility* (Bethany House, 2001), 32.
7. McKnight, Scot, *The Sermon on the Mount*, The Story of God Bible Commentary (Zondervan, 2013), 33.

Chapter 2

1. Brown, Francis, Samuel Rolles Driver, and Charles Augustus Briggs. *A Hebrew and English Lexicon of the Old Testament* (Hendrickson Publishers, 1996), 1022.
2. Andrus, Becki, "Sitting Shiva: What Is Shiva?" *My Farewelling* (no date). Available at: https://www.myfarewelling.com/article/sitting-shiva.
3. Oz, Frank (Director), *What About Bob?* (Touchstone Pictures, 1991).
4. DeYoung, Kevin, "Tim Keller on Reformed Resurgence" [Podcast] (February 1, 2021). Available at: https://rss.com/podcasts/lbe/775652/.
5. Kapic, Kelly M., *You're Only Human: How Your Limits Reflect God's Design and Why That's Good News* (Brazos Press, 2022), 64–71.

Chapter 3

1. Burge, Ryan P. *The Nones: Where They Came From, Who They Are, and Where They are Going* (Fortress Press, 2019).

2. Hancock, John Lee (Director), *We Crashed*, Episode 1 (Apple TV, 2022).
3. Zapata, Kimberly, "How to Manifest Anything You Desire," *Oprah Daily* (June 22, 2022). Available at: https://www.oprahdaily.com/life/a30244004/how-to-manifest-anything/.
4. Carter, Joe, "What You Should Know About the Prosperity Gospel," *TGC* (May 3, 2017). Available at: www.thegospelcoalition.org/article/what-you-should-know-about-the-prosperity-gospel/.
5. Weisman, S. (Director), *Waste Management, Inc.* Season 1, Episode 1, Undercover Boss (Studio Lambert, February 7, 2010).
6. The Greek word Matthew uses here for gentle is the same one he uses in Matthew 5:5 for meek.
7. Ortlund, Dane C., *Gentle and Lowly: The Heart of Christ for Sinners and Sufferers* (Crossway, 2020), 24.
8. Neville, Morgan (Director), *Won't You Be My Neighbor?* (Focus Features, 2018).

Chapter 4

1. Pennington, Jonathan T., *The Sermon on the Mount and Human Flourishing: A Theological Commentary* (Baker Academic, 2017), 89.
2. Keller, Timothy, *Counterfeit Gods: The Empty Promises of Money, Sex, and Power, and the Only Hope that Matters* (Dutton, 2009).
3. Mouritsen, Ole G. et al, *Umami: Unlocking the Secrets of the Fifth Taste* (Columbia University Press, 2014).
4. Davis, Jim and Michael Graham, *The Great Dechurching: Who's Leaving, Why Are They Going, and What Will It Take to Bring Them Back?* (Zondervan Reflective, 2023), 3, 24–25, 28.

Chapter 5

1. As believers, we often associate mercy solely with what we offer to those who have wronged us. However, mercy is wider than this and involves both making amends and meeting needs. Throughout this chapter, we use the terms mercy and compassion interchangeably.
2. "'Just Deserts' or 'Just Desserts'?" *Merriam-Webster Dictionary* (no date). Available at: https://www.merriam-webster.com/words-at-play/just-deserts-or-just-desserts.

3. Wilson, Timothy D., and Daniel T. Gilbert, (2005) "Affective Forecasting: Knowing what to want," *Current Directions in Psychological Science*, Vol 14, 131–134.
4. Carlsmith, K. M., T. D. Wilson, and D. T. Gilbert, (2008) "The Paradoxical Consequences of Revenge," *Journal of Personality and Social Psychology*, Vol 95, 1316–1324.
5. Ibid., 1316.
6. Ibid., 1320.
7. Ibid.
8. Hoover, Christine, *Messy Beautiful Friendship: Finding and Nurturing Deep and Lasting Relationships* (Baker Books, 2017).
9. Most of the names and details for other stories in this book have been changed for privacy reasons, but this story is shared with permission, just how it happened.
10. Keller, Timothy, *Forgive: How Should I and How Can I?* (Hodder & Stoughton, 2023).

Chapter 6

1. I (Elizabeth) was helped here by Courtney Doctor's illustration of ornamental and fruit-bearing pear trees for the relationship between faith and works throughout the book of James at The Gospel Coalition Conference for Women in 2021.
2. Pennington, Jonathan T., *The Sermon on the Mount and Human Flourishing: A Theological Commentary* (Baker Academic, 2017), 170.
3. Ibid., 81.
4. Bailey, Kenneth E., *Jesus through Middle Eastern Eyes: Cultural Studies in the Gospels* (InterVarsity Press, 2008), 83–84.
5. Pennington, Jonathan T., *The Sermon on the Mount and Human Flourishing: A Theological Commentary* (Baker Academic, 2017), 80.
6. Fujimura, Markoto, (2021) *Columbines—Hope* [artwork]. Available at: https://makotofujimura.com/art/portals/columbines.
7. Cipiti, Jonathan (Director), *Kintsugi—A Short Film* (Windrider, 2020). Available at: https://windriderbayarea.org/kintsugi/.

Chapter 7

1. Borg, Marcus J., and John Dominic Crossan, *The Last Week:*

What the Gospels Really Teach About Jesus's Final Days in Jerusalem (HarperOne, 2007), 3.

Chapter 8

1. Guthrie, Nancy, *Blessed: Experiencing the Promise of the Book of Revelation* (Crossway, 2020), 18.
2. "World Watch List Trends," *Open Doors* (2023). Available at: https://www.opendoorsus.org/en-US/persecution/persecution-trends/.
3. Guthrie, Nancy, *Blessed: Experiencing the Promise of the Book of Revelation* (Crossway, 2020), 112.
4. Lloyd-Jones, Martyn, *Studies in the Sermon on the Mount* (Eerdmans Publishing, 1976), 112.
5. We recommend Michael Hesiner's book *The Unseen Realm* for a lengthy discussion on the supernatural. We were also helped by The Bible Project's Spiritual Being Series, available at: https://bibleproject.com/explore/category/spiritual-beings-series/.
6. We were helped by the Bible Project's "Book of Revelation Summary: Part 1" available at: https://bibleproject.com/explore/video/revelation-1-11/.
7. This idea was made popularized by American psychologist, Carl Rogers.
8. Holleman, Heather, *The Six Conversations: Pathways to Connecting in an Age of Isolation and Incivility* (Moody Publishers, 2022), 29.
9. Bruner, Frederick Dale, *Matthew: A Commentary*, Vol 1 (Eerdmans, 2007), 181.

Conclusion

1. Pennington, Jonathan T., *The Sermon on the Mount and Human Flourishing: A Theological Commentary* (Baker Academic, 2017), 119.